Windsor
(Old and New)
a Thousand Years

Windsor
(Old and New)
a Thousand Years

WINDSOR LOCAL HISTORY
PUBLICATIONS GROUP

The picture on the front cover is a detail from
A View of Windsor High Street and Market by William Westall, c1830
and hangs in the Guildhall, Windsor.
It is reproduced by permission of
The Royal Borough of Windsor and Maidenhead

The photograph on the back cover is by George Henton
and is reproduced by permission of the Record Office
for Leicester Leicestershire and Rutland

The drawing on the back cover is of the Kingsbury Beast

Windsor Local History Publications Group was formed in 1976 from a small group of WEA students and tutors with the aim of fostering research in the field of local history and publishing the results.
Officers in 2001
Chair: Hester Davenport
Secretary: Beryl Hedges
Treasurer: Patrick Rooney

This book first published in March 2001
Reprinted (with corrections) April 2001
by Windsor Local History Publications Group
256 Dedworth Road Windsor SL4 4JR

Typeset by Pamela Marson
Cover by Colin Gray/ Ken J. Byerley
Printed in England by Antony Rowe of Chippenham, Wiltshire, England

ISBN 0 9505 567 5 0

In Memory of

Gordon Cullingham
and
Raymond South

Both founder members of
Windsor Local History Publications Group
who died in 1999

Acknowledgements

The Windsor Local History Publications Group owes a great debt of gratitude to Pamela Marson, editor of our journal *Windlesora*, who proposed the idea for this chronology, and who has worked assiduously to bring it into being. She has collated all the contributions and entered them on computer, and has personally undertaken a great deal of the research. She has found many of the illustrations, used her photographic skills to provide others, and formatted the whole book for the printer. The finished work is owed in very large part to her dedication and quiet resolve.

We are also much indebted to our Treasurer, Patrick Rooney, for his hard work in securing and overseeing the financing of the publication.

Editorial Committee

Hester Davenport, Beryl Hedges, Judith Hunter, Pamela Marson and Sheila Rooney

Contributors from the WLHPG

Valerie Bonham, Gordon Cullingham, Hester Davenport, Ellen Dollery, Margaret Gilson, John Handcock, Beryl Hedges, Judith Hunter, Jean Kirkwood, Jane Langton, Pamela Marson, Barbara Mitch, Patrick Rooney, Sheila Rooney, Joyce Sampson, Kerry Thomas, Kathleen Whelan.

Other Contributors

The WLHPG is grateful to a number of non-members for their written contributions, drawings, information, or practical help and advice:

David Alexander, Joan Ballhatchet, Valerie Batt-Rawden, Revd Louise Brown, Ron Boyle, Jane Burr, Elizabeth Counsell, Revd Jonathan Cruickshank, Olivia Davenport, Damaris Graham, Anthony Fanning, Daphne Fido, Gordon Franklin, Alexandra Freeman, Patricia Fullalove, Stephen Gilson, Olivia Gooden, Colin Gray, Leslie Grout, Colin Hague, Ron Hudson, Alan Jervis, Fraser Jansen, Cllr Karin Löhr, John Long, Geoff Messenger, Brigitte Mitchell, Olwen Mundye, Jacqueline O'Brien, Norman Oxley, Anthony Ray, Albert Shaw, Michael Trend MP, Geoffrey Try, Keith Watson, Neville Wridgway.

In addition we should like to thank the following for allowing us to reproduce pictures which they own: Clewer Local History Museum, Beryl Hedges, Oxford Blue, Anthony Ray, Convent of St. John the Baptist, Geoffrey Try, Record Office for Leicester, Leicestershire and Rutland, British Museum, Royal Borough Museum Collection, Windsor Library.

There are in addition many other citizens of Windsor, past and present, who have helped unwittingly and to whose work, if unacknowledged, we are indebted.

Above all we should like to acknowledge with great gratitude the grants we have received from the **Friends of the Royal Borough Museum Collection**, **The Prince Philip Trust**, the **Rotary Club of St. George**, **The Mayor's Benevolent Fund of the RBWM** and **The Windsor & Eton Society**, and the generous loan from the **Royal Albert Institute Trust**. We are likewise most grateful to the **Royal Borough of Windsor and Maidenhead** for granting us free access to and use of the **Royal Borough Museum Collection**, and for the privilege of launching the book in the Guildhall Chamber.

Contents

Foreword

By Michael Trend, MP for Windsor

Windsor is famous throughout the world for its magnificent castle. We know much about its construction and treasures; its history is well recorded. The castle has, rightly, been celebrated in countless ways.

Of the many distinguished artists who have worked at Windsor my favourite is Paul Sandby. He peoples his fine views of the castle with an everyday world going about its business. One shows the view from the old Town Gate looking down Castle Hill around 1765. Through the dilapidated structure we suddenly glimpse a scene in the town beyond. Men meet to talk over the concerns of the day. A cart has stopped and heavy luggage is manoeuvred. Beer is being delivered to one of the town's inns. In the foreground a child plays with its hoop.

This particular historical snapshot reminds us of the thriving, complex town that Windsor has always been. It has had an important life of its own which until recently was little studied. The Windsor Local History Publications Group has worked hard to remedy this. Its annual publication, *Windlesora*, is no respecter of persons. In its pages monarchs rub shoulders with lamplighters and laundresses; flying bombs and floods compete for attention with libraries and letterboxes.

In the present book we see more fruits of this approach to local history set in a broader context. Here are many more historical snapshots which, in their different ways, help to bring our local communities to life down the centuries.

At a time like our own, which seems to live only for the moment, those who gather and guard precious communal memories have a more vital task than ever. We learn much from piecing back together the carelessly discarded past. And we do well to remember that what may seem ephemeral today could be of the greatest fascination in years to come. Long may our local historians flourish.

Michael Trend.

Prologue

The First Thousand Years

AD 1 - AD 43

Two thousand years ago there was no town or village of Windsor. The Thames Valley was sparsely inhabited. Modern crop marks and archaeological excavations give us a glimpse of a landscape dotted with farmsteads, hamlets and woodland with a river not yet confined to its present-day course. The people who named the original settlement had not yet invaded this country, nor would they do so for another four hundred years. In the year AD 1 the people who lived here were Celts, Iron Age people or 'ancient Britons' as they have been called by some historians. They had migrated from the continent a century or so earlier. They were part of a widespread movement of people displaced by Roman activities and the westward migration of people from central and northern Europe. In their new homeland they retained some of their old allegiances and by the mid-1st century BC, Britain was divided into a large number of tribal areas.

The area we now know as Windsor was part of the Belgae Kingdom of the Atrebates, but we have little knowledge of the people who lived here. We might reasonably assume that the area closest to the river was inhabited but there have been only a few archaeological finds. However, long ago one gold stater from the reign of King Eppilus was found on St Leonard's Hill.

The Gold Stater from the reign of King Eppilus

Eppilus, much influenced by Roman culture, styled himself in Latin as REX CALLE - King of Calleva - on his coins. The site of Calleva, near Reading, is today occupied by the village of Silchester. But in the Roman period it was an important town, with a forum, shops, taverns, industry and a network of streets. It was the focus of several main Roman roads, one of which was to the south of Windsor and can still be traced in the landscape, a part of it is called the Devil's Highway. No doubt the road to Calleva was well known to the Celtic people living in the Windsor area, and the slap of hundreds of Roman sandals of marching soldiers, became a familiar sound.

The Roman occupation resulted in inter-tribal feuding. Eppilus's successor, Verica, deposed by the aggressively anti-Roman king of another tribe, fled to Rome in a last ditch attempt to regain his throne. He appealed to Emperor Claudius for help. But the eccentric, fifty-year-old Claudius had only recently become emperor and desperately needed an opportunity to gain military glory in order to consolidate his own position. So, the army he sent to Britain came not to help Verica, but to make Britain part of the Roman Empire.

AD 43 - AD 410

The Roman army landed in Kent in the summer of AD 43. By August several British tribes, including the Atrebates, had given in to Claudius without a fight. Triumphant, he returned to Rome leaving the army to set about making Britain a new Roman province. By AD 47 southern Britain had become a province of Rome, with the Atrebates a sub-servient kingdom and Calleva its administrative centre.

Britain remained part of the Roman Empire for almost 400 years, within which time, Calleva developed into an important town. The road from London crossed the Thames at Pontes (Staines), sweeping south of the present Windsor towards Calleva. A network of native roads already existed, and no doubt were extended or altered to accommodate the countryside under Roman and Romano-British cultivation. Almost certainly there were some settlements in the area of modern Windsor, be they villages or isolated farmsteads. As yet, however, there have been few finds from which to build a picture of Roman or Romano-British occupation of the area. Two tile tombs and a pottery kiln were found at Old Windsor and at St Leonard's Hill, the base of a Roman urn and ten coins spanning the period early second century to AD 375. We may not know much about the people who occupied the Windsor area during the four centuries of Roman rule, but we can be sure that they were here. In AD 407 the Roman army left Britain to fight in Gaul - never to return.

AD 410 - AD 835

Within a generation many Roman towns in Britain had ceased to function as urban centres and everywhere urban life was breaking down and with it Roman society. Local fighting and the neglect of roads and bridges weakened the function of the towns, while plagues and famine added to their downfall. In the countryside, the inhabitants fared only a little better, and hamlets and farmsteads reverted to a subsistence economy. And already another invasion had begun.

Unlike the Roman legions, the Anglo-Saxons did not come to Britain as soldiers in the pay of a mighty empire. They came as small groups of men intent on taking what they could in riches and land. They were at first raiders or mercenaries hired by a British leader to fight against other Saxons. There was no one decisive event comparable to the Roman invasion to mark their coming. It took almost two hundred years before Roman Britain could be called Saxon England. By the end of that period, however, the Saxon villages of Clewer, Dedworth and (Old) Windsor had been founded.

There are no written records to tell us their story. However, much can be deduced from their names, and from the sites they chose near the Thames and the wooded area which later became known as Windsor Forest. The name Dedworth is thought to mean the enclosure belonging to Dydda (or some such named person). Perhaps this refers to the green around which most of the houses lay until the early 19th century. It was one of several greens on the edge of the 'forest'. Clewer Green village had a similar location, but the main village of Clewer lay much closer to the Thames on a patch of slightly higher gravel which kept the houses above the winter floods. In due course the church and manor house were also built in this village. Its name, however, means the dwellers by the cliff, a reference to the chalk hill in their territory, which one day would become the site of a Norman castle. Whether there was ever a settlement belonging to Clewer on the chalk hill will probably never be known.

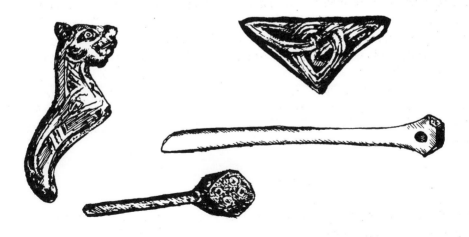

Finds from the Old Windsor Excavation: the 'Kingsbury Beast', a Triangular Gilt-Bronze Plate, a Bronze Pin and a Bone Bodkin

13

The riverside settlement of Windsor which was founded in Saxon times lay some two miles further downstream than the present town. Today it is known as Old Windsor. Excavations carried out in the 1950s revealed that the village had been established by the late sixth or early seventh century. Abundant archaeological finds illuminate the growth of the settlement. Most of the buildings were humble dwellings, but there was at least one substantial hall building which may have been used by Saxon kings from the ninth century onwards. By this date the settlement also had a water mill with three water wheels. Old Windsor must have been a place of some importance to warrant building on such a scale.

AD 835 - AD 1000

In AD 835 Vikings from Denmark overran the Isle of Sheppey. Scandinavian raiders had sporadically been raiding coastal settlements for some 50 years, but now in the 830s they became an ever-present and terrifying threat almost everywhere in Britain. The *Anglo-Saxon Chronicle* tells of many battles, ravaged countryside, burnt villages, and the uncertain peace brought about by Alfred the Great in 878. During the next hundred years, hostilities continued intermittently and in 994 the first payment of danegeld was made to the Danes to buy a temporary peace. Although we cannot know how much the raids and warfare affected the people living in Old Windsor, Clewer and Dedworth, a little can be imagined from references to other places in the local area, such as Reading and Thorney in Iver. One of Alfred's defences was built near Cookham and there are several entries in the Chronicle about the men of Berkshire paying danegeld and the county being invaded.

Saxon England was not one country but a conglomeration of rival kingdoms. Rivalries between them led to numerous changes of boundaries and at different times the Windsor area belonged to the kingdoms of Middlesex, Essex, Mercia and Wessex. From about the mid-9th century, however, it was part of Wessex, the most important of the kingdoms. It may be that by this date there was already a royal residence at (Old) Windsor and that Saxon kings were already enjoying hunting in Windsor Forest.

Judith Hunter

Bare Chalk Hill to Pilgrim Shrine

A thousand years ago there was no castle or town of Windsor under its walls. The Saxon town by that name lay two miles downstream and it was here that Edward the Confessor and other Saxon kings had a palace. The conquest of England by William of Normandy, however, brought great changes. About 1070 a castle was built on the nearby chalk hill overlooking the Thames Valley, on land which belonged to the Manor of Clewer. It was one of a ring of castles round London, erected to ensure the success of the Norman Conquest. It was a fort and a prison but it was Old Windsor which continued to be the place of occasional royal residence.

Walter Fitz Other was appointed the first Constable of the Castle. He also held Eton and several other manors, including Orton, which lay nearby. By the reign of Henry I the castle had become a palace with the king holding court there for the first time in 1110. The event is recorded in the *Anglo-Saxon Chronicle* which used the name New Windsor for the first time, to distinguish it from the original Saxon Windsor which now became officially referred to as Old Windsor. By 1130 a town had grown up to serve the needs of the castle. Almost certainly it was a planned town, but we can only speculate by whom it was planned - Henry I or perhaps the Constable of the Castle. Residents from the King's Manor of Old Windsor were no doubt encouraged to move to the new town and Old Windsor shrank in size and lost its town status.

For the first hundred and seventy years of its existence, New Windsor came under the jurisdiction of the castle. But by the mid-13th century the town had grown considerably in size and importance. Its streets and houses reached northwards to the river with its bridge and wharfs. It had its own church, and was a parish in its own right. In 1277 Edward I granted the town a charter, raising its status to that of a free borough which was responsible for its own affairs and taxes.

Charters of 1316 (Edward II), 1328 (Edward III), and 1379 (Richard II) confirmed the terms of the original charter, but in 1439 Henry VI granted a new charter in response to the depopulation and decline of the town. The charter gave the borough financial help and increased the power of civil and criminal jurisdiction over its inhabitants. This charter was confirmed in 1462 by Edward IV, who some years later, granted Windsor its third charter. The first surviving set of bye-laws dates from 1474. The impression of the town in the 13th and early 14th century gleaned from the charters and surviving deeds is of a small, but thriving community, with a merchants' guild out of which the town council would evolve. However, like many other towns and villages, Windsor suffered badly in 1348 when the Black Death swept across the country, heralding a period of decline. There were other years of plague which threatened the prosperity of the town, and in the 1360s townsfolk lost their rights to use common land east of the castle when the King took two hundred acres for a new deer park. This would appear to have been common land used for grazing animals and a source of chalk and flints. The period of depression lasted for some eighty years and an enquiry of 1439 revealed a depressing picture of a town which had become 'empty and wasted'. So much so that a petition to the King resulted in a substantial reduction to the borough tax. It took the coming of the Tudors to change the fortunes of the town to one of prosperity and a time of rebuilding.

Throughout the Middle Ages, Old Windsor and Clewer were separate parishes, each with its own parish church and villages at some distance from the town. In both parishes there would appear to have been two villages, one close to the church and the other round a village green. Local government was in the hands of their respective lords of the manor, who had power over the land and tenants of his manor. Dedworth was also a separate community which had grown up around a green, but its development was rather different. It did not become a parish and sometime in the Middle Ages it became divided; half of it became a detached part of New Windsor Parish (though not included in the borough), the other half, lying south of the Dedworth Road, became part of Clewer Parish. How and why this happened is not known, but it is probably connected to the fact that the manor became divided into Dedworth Maunsell and Dedworth Loring.

Separating the town and the several villages were fields and meadows. To the south lay the huge area of woodland, heath and marsh known as Windsor Forest. It was not devoid of habitation and there are numerous records of land being taken into cultivation and cottages erected. The Forest was as much a legal concept as an ecological one, an area subject to the laws of the forest and where the deer reigned supreme.

Judith Hunter

1000   There was no town of Windsor where we know it today but there was a place called Windsor two miles downstream and settlements at Clewer and Dedworth.

1011   The Danes overran Wessex, including Berkshire.

1061   The King, Edward the Confessor, ordained Aethelsige as the new abbot of St Augustine's Abbey at Canterbury; the ceremony took place at (Old) Windsor.

Edward the Confessor (1015-1066)

King Edward the Confessor was the son of Ethelred the Unready and Emma of Normandy. As England was largely in the hands of the Danes, Edward was sent to Normandy to be brought up as a Christian and from this he derived the name 'The Confessor'. He was noted for being a godly and abstemious man and was canonised in 1161.

He succeeded to the throne in 1042 at the age of 27 and was in many ways more Norman than Saxon. He seems to have favoured the settlement at Old Windsor because it was a convenient place for hunting in the extensive Windsor Forest. The royal building at Old Windsor, of which only archaeological remains survive beneath the fields, is variously described as a hunting lodge and a palace. Here the King 'wore his crown', making and administering law and here he is said to have performed a miracle, curing a blind man, Wulfin, by his touch. The unique dedication of Old Windsor Church to St Peter and St Andrew is said to have come about because Edward added his favourite, St Peter, to an earlier dedication to St Andrew.

Margaret Gilson

1066   *January* Edward the Confessor granted the manor of (Old) Windsor to the monastery of St Peter at Westminster.
The English were defeated at Hastings by William of Normandy.
William was crowned King of England. As King he now owned the manor of Clewer and soon acquired (Old) Windsor from St Peter's, Westminster.

c1070   A wooden castle was built on the chalk hill overlooking the Thames on land belonging to Clewer Manor. It was one of many castles ringing London and of strategic importance for maintaining control of the Thames Valley.

1086   King William ordered a survey of England to establish what was owed to him in taxes. The survey was compiled hundred by hundred, vill by vill, within each shire - a mammoth task. The written record is known as the Domesday Book and includes entries for Clewer, Dedworth, Windsor and two other manors which have long since ceased to exist, known as Orton and Losfield.

Collecting data for the Domesday Book

The Entry for Clewer in the Domesday Book

1107   *Easter* The Anglo Saxon Chronicle records that Henry I held Court at Windsor. This is the last time such courts were held at (Old) Windsor.

1110   *Whitsuntide* Henry I held his Court for the first time at Windsor Castle at New Windsor. This is the first mention of the name New Windsor.

1130   Henry I gave a virgate of land (approximately 30 acres) to William Fitz Walter, Constable of the Castle, in exchange for land taken into the town. This is the first reference to the town of New Windsor, which had been founded to serve the castle.

1168   Probable date of the foundation of the leper hospital for men and women known as St Peter Without - that is, not within the town. It was prudently set at a distance from both the town and the castle, on the edge of Windsor Forest.

1184   Windsor Church was given to Waltham Abbey in Essex, together with its chapel at Old Windsor. This is the earliest reference to the church and the wording of the grant shows that New Windsor had become more important than Old Windsor.

1191   The Bishop of Bath and Wells held an ecclesiastical court in Windsor Parish Church to settle a dispute between the monks of Canterbury and the Pope.

1193   Siege of Windsor Castle. Prince John attempted to seize the crown while his brother, Richard I, was on a crusade. For two months the barons and a multitude of knights and foot soldiers besieged the castle where John was in residence.

1215   King John presented the Hermitage of St Leonard with a new chaplain, Geoffrey de Meysi. This is the earliest known reference to the hermitage which was founded by Sir William de Braose. He quarrelled with the king and fled for his life while his wife and son were taken prisoner and his lands seized.

15th June King John set his seal to Magna Carta. King John was staying at the castle and from there went to Runnymede where he was forced to place his seal to the charter which is often regarded as the foundation of civil liberties.

1216   Windsor Castle was again under siege. King John had persuaded the Pope to annul the agreements made at Runnymede and the barons sought help from the King of France. The siege lasted three months and the castle took a severe battering. Much damage was also done to the town and Old Windsor.

1218   A new church was built at Old Windsor to replace the one destroyed by French mercenaries.

1219   Earliest known reference to the Vicar of St John's, the Parish of New Windsor. He was simply known as Alan.

1227   Work at last began on replacing the castle's timber palisade overlooking Thames Street. It had been badly damaged during the siege. This was the last section of the wall to be rebuilt in stone and the opportunity was taken to use the latest ideas in military technology, building three round towers which would withstand siege weapons. Several houses built against the old wooden wall belonging to townsfolk were demolished in the process and their owners were compensated.

Building a Norman Castle

1236   The earliest known reference to Windsor Bridge. It is not known when the bridge was first built but in this year it was repaired with timber from Windsor Forest.

1242   Henry III paid compensation to 'the good men of Windsor' who lost their houses when the new wall was built and a ditch made. Windsor Castle's permanent garrison consisted of nine knights, four archers and seven watchmen. They would have been supplemented by men from local manors, fulfilling the lord of the manor's obligation to the king.

1251   Warin is recorded as the name of the first known rector of St Andrew's Church, Clewer.

*The Font of
Clewer Church*

James Le Gaunter, the King's bailiff at Windsor, was appointed to keep the town with its market and heath. This is the first known reference to a market at Windsor.

1252   The hospital of St Peter's Without was granted 120 acres of land in Windsor Forest.

1268   Earliest record of an annual fair at Windsor. In fact, two annual fairs were held - on the vigils of St George, the patron saint of the chapel, and St John, the patron saint of the parish church, that is 23rd April and 24th June.

1272   A dispute as to whether a piece of cultivated land in Windsor Forest was in the Parish of New Windsor or Clewer, led to a visit by twelve knights and the establishment of the parish boundary.

1277   *28th May* **New Windsor was granted its first charter**: it now became a free borough responsible for managing its own affairs. This was a very important step in the development of the town. The Borough was granted the right to collect tolls (pontage) from those who passed over or under Windsor bridge for eight years. The tolls were for the repair of the bridge and over the years, grants of pontage were frequently made for the bridge was often in need of repair.

Earliest Borough Seal

1302   Windsor sent its first members to parliament. They were Thomas de Shaw and Henry de Bedford. One of the members for Berkshire was called Richard de Windsor.

1314   A petition was made to King Edward II asking that the county jail should be removed from Windsor. Amongst the reasons given were that Windsor was in the most remote part of the county and too small a town to provide food for the prisoners. After many years the jail was removed to Reading.

1321   Earliest record of John de Brocas purchasing land in Windsor. He eventually acquired a considerable estate and became Lord of the Manor of Dedworth and the newly created Manor of Clewer Brocas.

1344   *19th January* Townspeople may have found employment, and certainly had much to stare at, when all the nobles of England with their entourages were summoned to Windsor by King Edward III, for a great banquet followed by three days of jousting.

1348   *23rd April* **The Order of the Garter was instituted.**
The ceremonial initiated then, with service and procession of monarch and knights in dark blue robes, continues as a crowd drawing spectacle today. In contrast to the splendours of court ritual the devastating plague known as the Black Death cut short many lives.

Earliest record of choir boys at St George's Chapel being given schooling.

1350   Huge numbers of workmen were impressed into working in the castle to carry out Edward III's building programme - they must certainly have put a strain on the town's tradesmen for supplies and probably accommodation. The impressed workmen were employed for varying periods ranging from 11 to 144 days in any one year. Such conscripted labour continued to be used until at least the 1360s.

1355   Pope Innocent VI granted the hermitage of St Leonard the right to grant indulgences to pilgrims visiting and leaving alms. Indulgences were thought to shorten the time that pilgrims suffered in the fires of purgatory after death and before ascending to heaven.

1357   The poet Geoffrey Chaucer attended the Feast of the Garter as page to the Countess of Ulster. He was about fifteen years old at the time. Her records show that she bought him a jacket, new shoes, and some red and black stockings for the occasion.

1363   John Payntour became the first person to be known as the mayor of Windsor.

1369   First mention of a Guildhall in Windsor. It would have been the meeting place of the merchants' guild and, perhaps, later the meeting place of the town council which evolved from the guild.

1380   A handsome market cross was erected in the centre of the town by one John Sadler. It stood more or less on the site of Queen Victoria's statue.

1384   Sir Bernard Brocas founded the Brocas Chantry at St Andrew's Church Clewer. The southern aisle was converted into a chantry chapel and the income from land given by Sir Bernard provided a stipend for a chantry priest to say Mass daily for the souls of the founder and his family after their deaths.

1390   As Clerk of the King's Works to Richard II, Geoffrey Chaucer ordered a delivery of stone costing £100.17s.4d. for the repair of St George's Chapel as it was in danger of collapse.

1439   Windsor burgesses successfully petitioned the king, Henry VI, to reduce their taxes because the town had suffered 'great mortality and pestilence' at various times, and was now 'emptied and wasted' and its inhabitants were 'moneyless'. As a result the tax was reduced from £17 to £10. This period of recession partly explains why there are so few surviving medieval houses. The first record of justice being dispensed by the mayor in his capacity as a magistrate.

1444   The charter granted by Henry VI established the Corporation with its mayor, bailiffs and burgesses.

c1460   Edward IV created the Little Park to the east of the Castle on 200 acres of land where the townsfolk previously had the right to pasture animals and quarry chalk and flint.

A Powerful Knight

Sir Bernard Brocas was born in 1330 the third son of a Gascon, Sir John de Brocas, Seneschal of Windsor Castle, resident of Clewer and owner of much land in Windsor, Eton, Clewer, Dedworth, Dorney, Bray and Boveney. Sir Bernard was an important figure in the life of the Manor of Clewer in the fourteenth century. When King Edward III invaded France in 1346 he was accompanied by Sir John Brocas, his Master of Horse, and their respective sons, the Black Prince and his friend Bernard Brocas. On the shore at La Hogges, the Black Prince was dubbed knight and Bernard armed as Squire.

Sir Bernard married his second wife Mary, a widow and sole heiress to the Roches estates in 1361/2 and shortly afterwards accompanied the Black Prince and his wife to France where he was to serve as Constable of Aquitaine until 1366. He was then granted a very large pension of £50 a year and appointed first Master of the Royal Buckhounds which was an hereditary post. In 1369 he was elected Knight of the Shire and served in Parliament almost continuously until his death in 1395. He was Queen's Chamberlain and Captain of Castles.

In 1377, on the death of his nephew, Sir Bernard inherited the family estates of Beaurepaire. His wife Mary died in 1380 and he then married Katherine, widow of Sir Hugh Tyrell. In 1385, Sir Bernard endowed Clewer Church's Brocas Chapel as a Chantry Chapel for daily masses for the repose of the souls of Lady Mary Brocas and others. Chaplains continued to be appointed until 1546 when, following the Act for the Suppression of Chantries, the Rector of Clewer was appointed Chaplain and thus the old merged with the new. When Sir Bernard Brocas died in 1395 he was given an elaborate funeral and his fine embattled tomb occupies the chief place in St Edmund's Chapel in Westminster Abbey.

Joyce Sampson

1462 Edward IV granted the borough a new charter confirming a reduction in taxes on account of the great changes and losses which the town had sustained.

The leper hospital of St Peter was given to the newly founded Eton College. Leprosy was no longer a significant problem. Over the centuries the land belonging to the hospital proved to be a valuable source of income for the college.

1466 Edward IV granted the town a Charter of Incorporation. The new corporation consisted of a mayor, bailiffs, and burgesses, numbering in all not more than 30. From then for almost four centuries, Windsor was ruled by this self-perpetuating oligarchy. A few of the privileged elite of the town would elect members from amongst themselves.

1475 Work began on the re-building of St George's Chapel. Once again there was an influx of tradesmen. This meant an improvement in the fortunes of the town's merchants.

1478 The bones of John Schorn, vicar of North Marston in Buckinghamshire were brought to St George's Chapel where they attracted throngs of pilgrims who visited the shrine. Pilgrims were expected to leave alms - a useful source of income for Edward IV's building programme.

The Legend of Jack-in-the-Box

John Schorn, uncanonised saint, who lived in the thirteenth century, is reputed to be the first person to use a Jack-in-the-box. When he preached to his congregation he would conjure a devil out of a boot and instruct them how they could deal with the devil in their character. "Contain the devil in you as I contain the devil in this boot".

Martyrs and Mayhem

John Norden's map of 1607 gives a vivid glimpse of Windsor, a small market town which had grown little in extent since the thirteenth century, when it was first granted borough status. During the fifteenth century the town had suffered very badly from plagues and other misfortunes, but by the 1520s prosperity had returned to Windsor. The castle was one of the favoured royal residences bringing nobles, courtiers and business to the town. New houses were being built to replace the old and, as in many other towns and villages, red bricks were being used instead of wattle and daub; some of these houses can still be seen in the narrow streets opposite the new castle gate built for Henry VIII.

The parish church was enlarged, the Trinity Guild (the successor to the medieval merchants guild) built a new meeting place, probably leaving their old guildhall for the use of the corporation. A new market house was built in the High Street, and a private Act of Parliament allowed the corporation to pave the streets for the first time. The population grew and more houses were needed, but the town grew inwards, not outwards, with buildings lining the castle ditch. However, by modern standards it was still a very small town with a population of around a mere one and a half thousand, and less than two thousand at the Restoration in 1660.

The original borough had encompassed only part of the built-up area. The town houses of the easternmost part of Clewer Manor which lay between the bridge and the castle were not within its boundaries. Neither were the houses of Windsor Underore, a manor which lay to the north of the castle and belonged to Reading Abbey. In 1539 Reading Abbey was dissolved and the following year the area of the borough was considerably extended by the purchase of Windsor Underore. Surveys and deeds and John Norden's map of 1607 show a pattern of streets which can be recognised today, though some of their names have changed.

New charters confirmed the borough's rights to hold a weekly market, two fairs, and to manage its administrative and judicial affairs, including the regulation of trade. The corporation jealously safeguarded the rights of the borough's own traders against 'foreigners'. The mayor and corporation had a difficult task for Windsor, like most towns of the period, was faced with the problems of vagrancy, poverty, and ever-recurring plagues. The religious upheaval following Henry VIII's break away from Rome brought numerous changes to the town, including the suppression of its Trinity Guild and the burning at the stake of three Windsor men who dared to think for themselves. By the mid-seventeenth century, when the Civil War divided the nation, Windsor had become a puritan town that from the outset had supported the Parliamentary cause. Then as now, it was a garrison town, and soldiers were billeted on private houses as well as the town's many inns and alehouses. This brought great hardship for money to pay the army was often in short supply. This burden was not relieved until after the monarchy was restored in 1660.

Beryl Hedges

1489　The Treaty of Windsor was signed at Windsor Castle; it was between England and Portugal and makes Portugal our oldest ally.

1499　*4th July* Sir Reginald Bray, Chancellor of England and Knight of the Garter, bought the Manors of Clewer, Old Windsor and New Windsor. At his death he left money to be used specifically for the completion of St George's Chapel.
There was an outbreak of sweating sickness.

1501　Thomas Hunte's Charity was established. It is the earliest known charity in Windsor. He gave four houses with gardens in Sheet Street for eight poor persons, and land in Warfield for their support.

1510　The main gate to the castle was rebuilt and named the Henry VIII Gate.

1512　The last known mention of St Leonard's Hermitage in surviving records occurs in a conveyance of Clewer Manor.

The Hermit of St Leonard's Chapel

The Chapel of St Leonard's was a place of pilgrimage during the medieval period where pious Christians would visit the hermit who lived there to confess their sins and be forgiven. When William Caxton set up his printing press in 1476 one of the earliest pieces that he printed was 'Le Morte d'Arthur' by Sir Thomas Malory. This contained the story of Launcelot who, when training for a tournament, stayed with the hermit of St Leonard's and went daily to the neighbouring spring where 'he would lye down and see the well sprynge and burbyl'.

Sheila Rooney

1514 The earliest surviving corporation accounts date from 1514. They are part of the New Windsor Borough archives held at Berkshire Record Office.

1515 A ducking stool was made for the corporation at a cost of 7s 8d.

1518 A new meeting house was built for the Trinity Guild, the successor to the merchants' guild established in the 13th century. Today the building is the Three Tuns public house.

The Three Tuns in 2000

1519 The castle was still a favoured royal residence and attracted a great number of nobles and courtiers, so many that visitors were restricted as to the number of horses they were allowed to bring into the town.

1520 Henry VIII left Richmond on Garter Day, meeting his noblemen between there and Hounslow. They then rode together to Windsor, passing through Colnbrook, Upton and Eton, meeting Queen Catherine and the ladies of the Court in a field near to Windsor Bridge. The procession then went along Thames Street and through the main gate of the castle for the Garter Service.

1523   Windsor residents paid £178 tax to the Crown. Comparison with taxes paid by other towns suggests that prosperity had returned to Windsor. The town ranked as thirty-second in the country.

1529   The earliest known borough rental includes the names of at least 20 inns and alehouses, including the White Hart and the Mermaid Inns. Today these inns are known as the Harte and Garter and the Castle Hotel.

1536   A priest was hanged from a tree at Windsor Bridge and Mark Fytton (or Fitch), a butcher, on gallows in front of the castle gate, for having protestant views. They were both charged with treason, tried and executed on the same day. A cross carved near the foot of the Curfew Tower is thought to commemorate Mark Fytton.

The cross carved for Mark Fytton

1537   Henry VIII imprisoned the poet Henry Howard, Earl of Surrey, for a short time in the castle because of his quarrel with Lord Hertford.

1539   Reading Abbey was dissolved and its land and buildings passed to the ownership of Henry VIII. The abbey owned land in Windsor known as Windsor Underore which lay to the north of the castle. It was granted to a Thomas Ward and the following year his son Richard sold it to the corporation and Windsor Underore became part of the town.

Burnt at the Stake

The story of the **Windsor Martyrs** is told in *Foxe's Book of Martyrs*, and concerns five men - Anthony Pierson, Henry Filmer, Robert Testwood, John Marbeck and Robert Bennet - who were accused of being heretics. In 1539 an Act of Parliament was passed which 'abolished' diversity of religious opinion and enforced belief in six fundamental Catholic doctrines. Stephen Gardiner, the Bishop of Winchester, pursued anyone who questioned this long-accepted theology, or even by reading about the new ideas.

Anthony Pierson was a priest who was said to have preached "heretical" sermons in Windsor. Henry Filmer, a tailor and church warden, who thought that the vicar was preaching superstitious nonsense. Robert Testwood was in St George's choir and gave offence there when he criticised what he considered to be the exploitation of pilgrims. Gardiner had spies reporting to him and in March 1544 he persuaded King Henry VIII to allow for a search of heretical books. John Marbeck was a respected musician but during the search he was found to have words by John Calvin, which he had copied. Later in the month he was arrested with the others, including Robert Bennet, a Windsor lawyer. At the trial in Windsor on 26th July 1544 the jury was specially chosen from St George's tenant farmers, and all five were found guilty.

A royal pardon was granted to John Marbeck. It was thought that this was because the King admired his musicianship. Robert Bennet had been left in prison during the trial as he had the plague. When he recovered he lodged an appeal. The papers showed that there was no real evidence for any of the convictions. The King granted Bennet a pardon, and withdrew his favour from all those who had conducted the heresy hunts. But by then it was too late for Pierson, Filmer and Testwood, who had been burnt at the stake on waste-ground below the Castle on 28th July 1544.

Jean Kirkwood

1547   Henry VIII was buried at Windsor Castle as it was his wish to be buried next to Jane Seymour, his third wife and mother of his only son, Edward VI. The mayor was paid 42s 4d for cleaning the streets along which the funeral cortege would pass. Other towns on the funeral route were similarly treated.

1547   King Edward VI suppressed chantries and guilds, including the Holy Trinity Guild of Windsor and the Brocas Chantry at St Andrew's Church, Clewer. The chapel itself was not destroyed.

1551   John Aldem, a brewer, leased the Crown Inn from St George's Chapel – the Chapel owned six inns in Windsor. The property was leased by members of the Aldem family until 1615 and at sometime during this period the inn was converted to a brewery.

1554   Queen Mary and her new husband, King Philip of Spain, the mayor and corporation processed along Peascod Street on the occasion of the installation of King Philip as a Garter Knight.

1555   Piped water from Winkfield provided the castle with a new source of water and a fountain.

1560   Windsor shoemakers petitioned the town council concerning the 'foreign' shoemakers who came to town on market days. Those who lived in the town had to pay taxes, while those who lived outside did not. Over the next few years the council came to agreements with various trades: 'foreigners' should not be allowed to trade in certain areas of the town and should pay a fee. Local traders had to prove they were good craftsmen and those who produced inferior goods would be treated as 'foreigners'.

Host of the Garter Inn

Richard Gallys was a rich burgess who, it is thought, was the model for Shakespeare's host in *The Merry Wives of Windsor* which was written c1597. Gallys was mayor of Windsor three times between 1561 and 1573 and was elected an MP in 1562. At his first attendance at parliament he (rather unwisely) moved that a suitable husband should be found for Queen Elizabeth. He was re-elected in 1572 but died on St Andrew's Day in 1574 when he was 68 years old. He was buried in the middle of the south aisle of the old parish church at Windsor. He had a wife, Alice, ten sons and two daughters. On the brass that covered his grave it is recorded that he was learned, and lived a godly life (this does not sound like Shakespeare's mine host!). He did many charitable deeds and commendably executed the office of mayor. In his will he left £30 to help the poor.

Pamela Marson

1561   A second borough rental lists the Garter Inn and its landlord, Richard Gallys.

1563   The *Book of Martyrs* by John Foxe was published with the story of the Windsor Martyrs as told by John Marbeck. The woodcut illustration shows the burning of Filmer, Testwood and Pierson.

Drawing shows part of the woodcut which depicts the story of the Windsor Martyrs

1566   New heraldic arms were granted to the Borough of New Windsor, depicting
        the castle and a deer's head representing the park and forest.

Arms from Sixteenth Century Manuscripts

1574   Richard Gallys left £30 to the corporation to buy land to provide an income for
        helping the poor. His son, John Gallys, citizen and goldsmith of London, gave
        an additional £300.

1575   Another endowment enabled the Franklyn Almshouses to be built in Moor
        Street (now Park Street).
        A pest house was built in Sheet Street for plague victims. Until that time they
        had been forced to live in 'hutches' in Worth Field.
        The Windsor Parish Church was enlarged and a gallery was built for the
        mayor, aldermen and other burgesses.

The Michell family of Old Windsor

Humphrey (died 10th October 1598), Frances (died 13th May 1621) and Samuel (died 15th March 1613) are commemorated in Old Windsor Parish Church by fine brasses now mounted on the south wall. **Humphrey Michell** came to Windsor from Yorkshire to work at the castle in the reign of Elizabeth I. In 1570 he became an MP for Windsor and in 1572 he was appointed Clerk of the Works at the castle. Over several years he supervised a considerable programme of repair and building at the castle. In 1576 he was granted the reversion of the estate known as Waltons where he lived. Today it is known as Woodside. Frances was his second wife and Samuel his second son - her first. Samuel continued the tradition of service to the Crown becoming Marshal of the Hall to King James I.

Margaret Gilson

1576   The plague came to Windsor and lasted more than a year.

1577   Lists of innkeepers, taverners and alehouse keepers were drawn up by orders of the government because it was proposed to tax each of them to raise money for the repair of Dover Harbour. The document records that Windsor had 8 inns, 5 taverns and 8 alehouses. Clewer and Old Windsor had one alehouse each.

1585   An Act of Parliament gave the borough the authority to pave its streets with cobble stones. Previously the streets had been 'yearly impaired and made noisome and foul by reason of the great and daily carriage and re-carriage' to her Majesty's Castle.

1586   Queen Elizabeth was received by the mayor and corporation in the Guildhall (the old Guildhall in Church Street) when she made a state entry to Windsor Castle.
A new Market House was planned. Much of the money needed was raised by the mayor, bailiffs and burgesses cutting down their expenses. Money that would have been spent on dinners was paid towards the building fund. Several gifts were also received, including 40s. from the Earl of Leicester.

1591   The new market house was completed.

1597   *May* Lord Henry Hunsdon, patron of Shakespeare's acting company, the Lord Chamberlain's men, was installed as a Knight of the Garter. He swept up the hill to the ceremony with a train of 300 men dressed in his livery of orange taffeta. *The Merry Wives of Windsor* is believed to have been written to celebrate this event, and was probably first played in front of Queen Elizabeth either at Whitehall or, as tradition has it, in Windsor.

'Now, good Sir John, how like you Windsor wives?'

In *The Merry Wives of Windsor* (c.1597), Sir John Falstaff is three times fooled by the lively wives, Mistress Page and Mistress Ford. These are surnames found among Windsor citizens then, and traditionally Master Ford's house was thought to be among those lining the castle ditch opposite the Garter Inn where scenes in the play are set. **Shakespeare** is always associated with his birthplace, Stratford-upon-Avon, yet it is his Windsor play which conveys a topographically-accurate sense of place. Not only the town, but the Great Park, a Frogmore farm, Old Windsor, Eton and Datchet are featured. When Falstaff hides in a laundry basket, Mistress Ford tells her servants to carry it to Datchet Mead and empty it 'in the muddy ditch close by the Thames-side'. The playwright clearly knew the area, and knew too that it was not just dirty clothes which might find their way into the river, but all the town's rubbish. The dripping Falstaff laments that he was dumped there 'like a barrow of butcher's offal'. To warm his cold belly he calls for a quart of sack (sherry) at the Garter Inn. It is surely not too fanciful to imagine that the playwright could sometimes be found on its benches, quaffing and quipping with the locals.

Hester Davenport

1603   James I granted Windsor a new charter which confirmed the borough's right to hold a weekly market and a Court of Pleas.

The Bishop of Salisbury's terrier for this year, which lists all the land owned by the bishop, refers to Clewer Rectory as 'lately built'; it was demolished in 1963.

There was a bad outbreak of plague between July and November. The average monthly death rate was 26.6 in contrast to the normal rate of less than five.

In his will Thomas Needham left two properties near Windsor church, the income from which was to be used to buy bread weekly to be given to twelve poor persons.

1604   A new pest house was built at the lower end of Sheet Street, on a site recently purchased by Thomas Aldem for this purpose. This building was later used as a workhouse.

1607   John Norden was commissioned by James I to make an atlas depicting Windsor Forest and parks in the Windsor area. His map of the Little Park (now the Home Park) includes the earliest view of the town. This shows that the street pattern of the 17th century has changed little today. The market house, pillory and whipping post are also depicted – but not the old market cross.

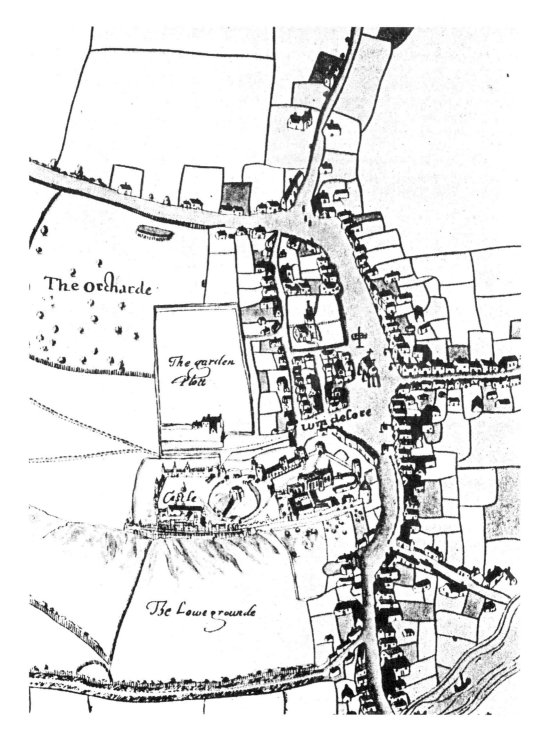

John Nordens Map of 1607

1610   The bye-laws of this year ordered that hedges and ditches should be kept in good repair. Residents of the town were now beginning to show some pride in the condition of the roads.

1612   A new pillory was made by Roger Printer.

1613   Edward Vaughan left £20 in his will for the use of poor.

1614   Mrs Agnes Urmston gave £50 for the use of six poor widows of Windsor or Eton. It should be remembered that widows often became destitute on the death of their husband if they were not provided for.

1618   All the innkeepers and alehouse keepers of Windsor were required to make a bond with the magistrates that they would not serve meat dishes during Lent. 15 innkeepers and 19 alehouse keepers did so.
        This same year Sir Giles Mompesson exercised his monopoly to license inns in Windsor – however, only Richard Croxford of the White Hart paid the £5 demanded.

1621   Dr Robert Challenor gave some property at East Oakley, Fifield and Bray to produce an income of £6 at Lady Day and Michaelmas to be given to twelve of the 'godliest' poor.
        Andrew Windsor gave £200 to buy stock for the poor to make cloth.

1623   A very severe plague started which lasted until 1625.

1626   Three shops were built in castle ditch on the west side of Thames Street.

1629   John Dean, aged eight, was convicted and hanged in Abingdon for setting fire to two outhouses of the Garter Inn.

1630   There were complaints that townsfolk stole from the pipes bringing water to the castle from Winkfield. There was an acute water shortage in the town.

1633   The king's arms in the Windsor Parish Church was taken down. A new vestry was built for the church, the chancel was paved and wainscoted, and the altar was once again set at the eastern end of the chancel.

1635   The medieval market cross was restored, and, at the expense of Dr Godfrey Goodman, Bishop of Gloucester and Canon of St George's, it was beautified by the addition of a painted crucifix.

1635   New bye-laws were issued including:
cont.   *Every shopkeeper should maintain and repair the pavement near his shop.*
Every mayor should nominate a scavenger to remove rubbish from the pavements.
Pigs should not be allowed to run in the streets.
Dunghills and other obstructions should be removed from the streets.
Date of the earliest surviving Hall Book of the Borough of New Windsor. It is a record of the business of the town council or corporation.

1636   A whipping post was set up by the bridge.
According to John Taylor, author of *The Taverns in the Ten Shires About London*, Windsor had four taverns – the Cross Keys, Garter, George, and White Hart. These would have been wine bars within the inns.

1637   Richard Mitchinor was paid £4 for digging a new well to the south of the market house.

1640   The townspeople successfully challenged the corporation's monopoly of the electoral privilege of choosing the town's two members of parliament.
Archbishop Laud gave £50 to establish a charity to help poor boys to be apprenticed and to aid poor girls about to be married.

1642   The new crucifix on the market cross was removed because Windsor had become a Puritan town. During the Civil War the Windsor people sided with Cromwell and the Parliamentarians.
October Parliamentary troops took possession of the castle and Windsor was made the headquarters of the New Model Army with Colonel John Venn the Constable of the Castle.
7th November The Royalists under the command of Prince Rupert attacked the castle. There was some damage to the town but the castle remained in Parliamentary hands.

1643   Some 16,000 foot soldiers and 3,000 horsemen, who had been quartered around Windsor, marched to Reading, though one infantry regiment and a troop of horses under Colonel Venn remained permanently in the town at a cost of £3,000 a month.
Soldiers quartered at Windsor committed 'sad depredations' in the Great Park, and in the following year soldiers destroyed all the deer (about 500) in the Little Park and burnt the pales.
Dr Godfrey Goodman's crucifix was demolished.

1644   The King's silver was seized at Whitehall to pay for the garrison at Windsor, but in November a riot broke out at the castle because the soldiers were said 'to be in great want'.

1645   The New Model Army gathered in Windsor during March and April. The townspeople were dissatisfied with the quartering of soldiers on their already crowded town. The townsfolk had to pay taxes and levies for the maintenance of the army, but their own bills were not paid.
30th April The New Model Army left Windsor with some 22,000 men and marched to Reading.

1648   *June* There were fears that Royalists would attempt to seize Windsor Castle using the midsummer fair as a cover for filling the town with supporters, but nothing occurred.
24th November Windsor became the headquarters of the Parliamentary Army under Colonel Henry Ireton. In meetings at the castle and the Garter Inn the Council of Officers resolved to bring the King, imprisoned on the Isle of Wight, to trial.
15th December When the King was told he would be brought to Windsor, he declared himself pleased, as 'Windsor was a place he ever delighted in'.
20th December The King reached the town under armed guard. There was no official welcome or ringing of bells, but the townsfolk crowded to watch, crying 'God bless your majesty, and send you long to reign'. Royalists were said to be gathering and drinking the King's health in the town inns, so the garrison was reinforced, with several troops of horse stationed nearby.

1649   *19th January* The King left Windsor for his trial in London in a coach and six, 'a guard being made all along of muskets and pikes; both officers and soldiers expressing civility as he passed by; and at the great gate a party of horse, commanded by Col. Harrison, was drawn up in the market place at Pease-cod-street End'. The trial began at Westminster Hall the next day.
30th January King Charles I was executed at Whitehall.
9th February The body of the King was brought back to Windsor. Snow fell on the black pall covering the coffin as it was borne into St George's Chapel for burial, conducted without the benefit of a proper service. His burial was entered in the parish register.

1649   Windsor Bridge was practically rebuilt. Tolls were levied for transport using the bridge and for boats passing under it. This repair lasted until 1676.

1650   The organ was removed from the church – a dramatic assertion of puritan practices.

1653   The Borough Sessions Court fined all the town's innkeepers and alehouse
        keepers 3s 4d for selling by 'small measures'. It is likely that the corporation
        had recently purchased a new set of weights and measures. According to the
        records there were now 18 innkeepers and 26 alehouses keepers who were
        listed by name, including 12 who were unlicensed.
        Mrs Margaret Osborne gave £25 to form a stock of corn and coals for the
        poor. The corporation added £10.

1657   Cromwell visited Windsor, the corporation expending £1 1s 9d on
        entertainment.

1660   A justice of the peace commanded that a number of poor women and children
        should leave the castle before Charles II could take up residence. They were
        probably the families and camp followers of parliamentary soldiers who had
        been quartered in Windsor during the Civil War.

Hogs in the Street to Balloons in the Sky

The story of this period is of the slow transformation of a small, scruffy market town to something more urban and cosmopolitan, on the verge of the railway age and the beginnings of flight.

A time traveller alighting from his machine in Windsor of 1660 might well think that he was in a much earlier age, surrounded by timber-framed buildings and in streets where pigs rooted round piles of rubbish. But change came soon, and the destruction by fire of Shakespeare's Garter Inn in 1681, though accidental, could symbolise a turning from the past, while the new Guildhall of 1687-90 celebrated the future. It was built in the newly-fashionable classical style, mainly in red brick (older properties disguised their out-dated timber framing under coats of plaster).

When the traveller Celia Fiennes climbed the Round Tower in 1698 she commented on the number of fine gentlemen's houses she could see. These would have included Burford Lodge, built for Nell Gwyn on what had been a royal vineyard (it was now the home of her son by Charles II, the Duke of St Albans), and Pilgrim Place off Peascod Street, another grand house, with a garden with statues and fountains. Celia could also have noticed slum areas developing behind Thames Street. The problem for Windsor, then as later, was that the number of poor was growing, since there was little employment outside the brewing which went on down by the river. It was hard to escape the poverty-trap as few could read or write, though a Free School was established in 1705 for 70 poor children, of whom 30 were girls. For more than a century this was Windsor's only school.

By the end of the eighteenth century the population had increased and matters had got worse; Charles Knight, publisher and philanthropist, wrote in his autobiography of the 'misery of the poor in my native town' during his childhood then. The situation was exacerbated by the war with France (which lasted on and off from 1793-1815), which pushed up the price of bread and had to be financed by the introduction of numerous taxes. Charitable efforts at relief were made, with alms distributed and doles of bread given out at the church door. Knight reports a soup-kitchen set up in an empty house which helped fill empty stomachs, but the wretchedness which he observed in the early years of the nineteenth century turned the young man into a 'sort of Communist'. The hovels of the poor have long gone, but housing for the well-to-do, such as the eighteenth-century terraced houses of Park Street, still give character to the town, though their elegance may give a distorted sense of what life in Windsor was like at their time of construction. In Old Windsor too, members of the gentry built large mansions which contrasted with farm-workers' poky, insanitary cottages nearby. Two eighteenth-century examples in differing architectural styles are Beaumont Lodge on Priest Hill with its magnificent classical portico, and the gothic extravaganza near the river which Richard Bateman developed and named The Priory. His estate attracted visitors, which may have contributed to the nearby churchyard, noted for its fine trees, becoming a fashionable place for burials. Another drawn to Old Windsor was Princess Elizabeth, George III's daughter, who bought a property on the Priory estate in 1808; like her father she enjoyed farming and took great pride in the Chinese pigs which she bred there.

Ups and downs in the town's fortunes generally followed the presence or absence in it of Majesty. For Charles II Windsor was a place to take his pleasure, whether hunting or whoring, but he also restored the castle and St George's Chapel after the depredations of the Civil War, and created one of Windsor's most distinctive features, the Long Walk. Queen Anne gravelled over this grass walk, to make it easier for her two-wheeled hunting chariot which she drove through the Park at a furious pace. She lived more soberly, not in the castle but in her 'little box', a small house on the castle's southern side. George I and George II had no affection for Windsor, but it became the favourite home of George III. Hogs had to be driven from the town to prepare it for his first visit, but after he became resident the streets were properly paved and better lit, and under his patronage trade flourished. His son, George IV, had little interest in the town, but the dramatic alterations to the castle, including raising the height of the Round Tower, which was begun in his reign and completed under William IV, gave Windsor the appearance and silhouette by which it is recognised around the world today.

For almost the whole of this period the council responsible for local administration took its authority from the charter granted to the borough by Charles II. There were no elections as today: new members were co-opted by the existing body and expected to serve for life. From among the most senior members, the aldermen, a mayor was chosen turn by turn. It was not necessarily a welcome appointment but one to be accepted: in 1767 when Thomas Rutter was asked to serve for a fourth term he refused in 'contemptuous' terms, and was consequently fined. The recorded occupations of these local worthies (all men of course) show that most were involved in trade or service industries. To take only *abc* examples, there were apothecaries, attorneys, barbers, blacksmiths, brewers, butchers, carpenters, clockmakers, collar-makers, coppersmiths, and many more like them, engaged mainly in controlling trade and keeping the town clean and orderly. But council records show that stemming the tide of filth flowing through the streets was a task almost as impossible as controlling the sea's surges. Another perennial headache was the maintenance of the wooden bridge which connected Windsor with Eton. It was rebuilt in 1824.

Though there were disputes about council members, choice of candidates for parliament was much more contentious. In 1660 Windsor returned four MPs, two chosen by the council and two by citizens paying 'scot and lot' (parish rates), but from 1690 parliament decreed that there should only be two, chosen by the citizens. Elections were rowdy affairs, conducted by open, not secret, ballot. Bribery was rife and results routinely challenged; in 1778 even King George III was guilty of paying large sums to local tradesmen to get his own man elected. But from 1806 elections were peaceful, with one MP chosen by the court and one by the town. The Reform Act of 1832 brought back contested elections with a widened electorate, but did not stop the buying of votes. Three years later the Municipal Reform Act ended the closed, self-perpetuating local councils, establishing citizens' elections, all (male) rate-payers of three years standing having the vote.

At this time public office was denied to anyone other than a member of the Church of England. No longer did men go to the stake for their beliefs, but prejudice remained against Roman Catholics, Jews and non-conformists. In 1742 rabble rousers attempted to prevent the Methodist John Wesley from preaching in Windsor. Slowly tolerance grew, though theatre-loving Windsorians were dismayed when a group of dissenters (later known as Congregationalists) took over the Theatre Royal for their chapel in 1807. In 1816 a Methodist chapel was established, and in 1826 the Catholics finally acquired a place of worship. As the parish church had become dilapidated it could have seemed that the new forms of worship were usurping the old, but in 1822 Anglicans celebrated the consecration of a new church, whose graceful tower is a feature of the High Street today.

Religious worship occupied most Windsorians on Sundays but the town did not lack fun and games on weekdays, including bull-baiting and cock-fighting which seem barbarous today. The biggest jamboree was probably the celebration of King George III's Golden Jubilee in 1810, marked by an obelisk still found on Bachelors' Acre, but there were also firework displays and the thrice-yearly fairs with their bands of strolling players. In September 1831 thousands crowded into the Royal Mews and climbed onto roof-tops to watch a manned flight in a hydrogen balloon.

During these years Windsorians became increasingly aware that to outsiders their town was in itself an amusement. Guides were published from 1743 and visitors came from far and wide, though in 1782 the German Carl Philip Moritz found the inns far from welcoming. But walking by the river he was encouraged by 'a pair of red-cheeked young apprentices' to cast off his clothes and dive in with them. This was a pleasure which tourists and townsmen could enjoy alike, and for free.

Hester Davenport

1660   *12th May* To the sound of a trumpet King Charles II was three times proclaimed monarch, from the Market House, the bridge, and lastly from the Castle Gate. He was to become a habitual resident of the castle, his arrival in the town always celebrated by the ringing of the church bells.

It took time to restore normal life. Church silver, which had been stored in the town hall during the Civil War, was returned to the parish church, but 300 soldiers remained billeted on 38 Windsor innkeepers who petitioned parliament for redress (there is no evidence that they had success). At the borough's petition the Justice of the Peace was ordered to take care of the women and children who were ordered out of the castle.

The old mace was taken apart and 63 ounces of silver plate added.

1661   All holders of municipal office were required to take oaths of allegiance and supremacy. Corporation officials had to be members of the Church of England and take the sacrament of bread and wine to qualify for office.

Parliament decreed that of Windsor's four MPs only the two elected by the mayor and corporation could sit. Other citizens lost their representation.

1662   *14th July* The Crown's commissioners removed four of the council of 30 from office.

1663   Hearth tax was introduced. The amount paid by each town can be used to indicate the comparative prosperity of towns - Windsor ranked 44th.
In an attempt to tidy the town citizens were ordered to sweep up the 'soyle' before their doors.

Windsor petitioned unsuccessfully for a new charter to enshrine formally the sole right of the mayor and corporation to select the town's MPs.

1664   Payments were made for restoring the town's pillory and ducking stool.

9th February Bells were rung to celebrate the granting of a new charter. The boundaries were defined to include the hamlet of Dedworth and parts of Clewer.

The portrait of Charles II on the new charter

1665   In this year the Great Plague ravaged London, and claimed victims in Windsor too. Payments are recorded to soldiers for work done to repair the pest house where the sick were isolated. One Rose Burtal was paid half-a-crown for cleansing the house, and for supplying it with faggots, pitch, frankincense, brooms and candles. The corporation gave loans to those who could not afford to pay for laying out their dead.

1666   *26th February* The diarist Samuel Pepys and his wife visited Windsor to see the Chapel and the castle, which he called the 'most romantique castle that is in the world'. They lunched at the Garter Inn.

Viscount Mordaunt was dismissed from his post of constable of Windsor Castle for 'persecuting' William Tayleur, a barrister who had held the offices of Paymaster and Surveyor of the Castle, and was one of Windsor's MPs.

Following the Great Fire of London several dispossessed people arrived in the town and church records show charitable payments to some who 'had lost all by the ffier'.

1667   A hundred or more dissenters met regularly at the house of Samuel Price at Frogmore, which was at that time a hamlet close to the Little Park.

1668   Prince Rupert's appointment as Constable of the Castle and High Steward of Windsor was celebrated in the town with a bonfire and a banquet. The Prince began to oversee repairs to the castle, described then as 'exceedingly ragged and ruinous' by John Evelyn.

Monthly meetings of Quakers were established.

The widow Goring was paid for supplying padlocks and keys, a chain and a staple, for the whipping post.

1669   The earliest mention of a postal service in Windsor.

Several citizens were fined by the churchwardens for swearing or for 'being in an ale-house on a Sabbath day'.

1670   A licence was granted for the holding of Presbyterian services at the house of Mrs Jane Price, Samuel's widow, at Frogmore.

An allowance of 1s 6d a day for food, fire and candles was instituted by the King for guards quartered in Windsor, of whom there were three companies.

1672   Elias Ashmole, the Windsor Herald, visited the town and held a meeting in the Three Tuns public house. He was checking on the right of people to display heraldic arms. This is the earliest reference to the old Trinity House being used as an up-market alehouse.

c1672   A stagecoach service between London and Windsor was established. The watermen, who had previously carried all goods and passengers, were not pleased.

1674   *August* Prince Rupert organized a lavish re-enactment of the recent successful siege of Maestricht beneath the north terrace of the castle. The performance was attended by Samuel Pepys and John Evelyn, who called it 'a formidable show'. For many years thereafter that piece of land was known as Maestricht.

The White Lion Inn in the Market Place was used as a post office. The site is now part of Caleys department store, adjacent to the Castle Hotel. Letters were received from Maidenhead, the nearest place on the Bristol Road. A postal service was established between the general post office in London and Windsor, but only while the King was at the castle. This year he came on seven occasions, recorded through payments to the bell-ringers.

1676   Windsor had the highest number of protestant dissenters in Berkshire, 115 out of 1,025 adults.

25 loads of timber were ordered for the repair of the bridge.
The town well was repaired and cleansed at a cost of £2. 4s. 9d.

1677   The mayor and corporation liked to wine and dine. In this, as in other years, payment is recorded for 'the venison dinner'; there was also a dinner to be paid for when the mayor and some of the corporation went 'a-ffishing', while the marriage of Princess Mary and William of Orange was celebrated with a bonfire, and toasted in wine, beer and ale.

1678   Trouble flared up over how many MPs Windsor should have, and the right of citizens to elect their own.

1679   Citizens were again allowed to elect their own MPs.

Charles II gave Burford House to Nell Gwyn. Their son, the Duke of St Albans and his heirs, gave their name to St Albans Street, and played an important role in local affairs.

Nell Gwyn's Descendants

The **Dukes of St Albans** were dominant figures in eighteenth-century Windsor. The first Duke was the son of Charles II and Nell Gwyn. He gave his name to St Albans Street where he lived in Burford Lodge, the house presented to his mother, and he became High Steward of the town. This office was held successively by his son and then his grandson, though this third Duke ceased to live in the town after he had sold Burford Lodge to George III in 1777.

Four of the first Duke's sons represented Windsor in Parliament between 1722-54, and Lords Vere, Sidney and George Beauclerk were active members of the Corporation. Lord Sidney Beauclerk was notably personable. According to Lady Mary Wortley Montagu he was possessed of all his grandmother's 'beauty, wit and good qualities...Nell Gwyn in person with the sex altered'. He served as mayor in 1740-41 and as MP from 1733 until his death in 1744. Lord Sidney exercised his charm on Richard Topham (MP from 1698-1713), a wealthy man who became godfather of his only son, Topham Beauclerk, and who left Pilgrim Place, a fine house in Peascod Street, to Lord Sidney. This property afterwards passed to Topham. He also played a part in the town's local government and was elected to the Corporation in 1761. Another with his great-grandmother's wit and gaiety, he became a friend of the great Dr. Samuel Johnson whom he entertained at Pilgrim Place in 1752. With his death in 1780, having previously sold his properties in Windsor and Old Windsor to Sir Edward Walpole, the Beauclerks disappeared from Windsor life.

Hester Davenport

1680   The Long Walk was planted - a 240 foot wide avenue of elm trees running from the castle into the Great Park. It was used by the King for ease of access when hunting.

1681   *16th July* Sir Samuel Morland demonstrated his lately-invented water engine, which threw a jet of water over the castle. The King ordered it to be set up at Romney.

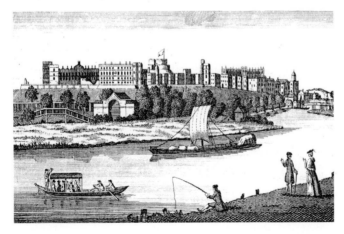

The Engine House is shown on this engraving of the castle

1681 But in 1681 there was no water supply at the top of the town when the White
cont. Hart and Garter Inns burnt to the ground. Prince Rupert as Constable of the
Castle organized the fire fighting, and since this was then mainly concentrated
on pulling down blazing buildings to prevent the fire spreading to others his
efforts must be seen as successful.

1682 A new White Hart was built on the site of the two burnt-out inns. £1 a year
rent was paid for encroachment of the new inn onto the pavement.

1683 Byelaws were passed to forbid anyone carrying on a retail business within the
borough unless they were a freeman (either through birth or after seven years
apprenticeship). The general uncleanliness of Windsor is shown in further
bye-laws which laid down that no one could keep hogs in the streets 'because
of the noisomeness of them', nor should anyone 'cause to be made dunghills
in the said street'. Rotting fish and vegetables were not to be thrown out
either. Householders were ordered to hang candles outside from Michaelmas
to Lady Day for street lighting.

1684 *2nd July* A week of cock-fighting at Windsor, organised by 'two persons of
quality', was announced in the *London Gazette*. It was a popular sport with
gamblers.

1685 *9th February* Gun salutes, bell-ringing and bonfires greeted the accession of
James II.
23rd March One of the King's first acts was to grant a new charter to
Windsor. The town was made a free borough with the same powers and
constitution as before.
18th June Following the suppression of the rebellion of the Duke of
Monmouth (bastard son of Charles II) his hatchments were removed from the
Garter Chapel and kicked into the castle ditch. Lord Jeffreys (Judge Jeffreys
of the 'Bloody Assizes'), who under the charter had been made Borough
Recorder, came to town. He left 'carnage, mourning and terror behind him' in
the west.
3rd July The Pope's nuncio arrived in Windsor for an audience with the King
and Queen. His entourage consisted of 36 coaches, each drawn by 6 horses.
Windsor citizens were said to be astonished by the influx of people, many of
whom found it difficult to obtain lodgings or provisions.

1686 Information was collected by local excise officers about the number of guest
beds and stables for horses available in every town and village. The statistics
were required for possible billeting of soldiers. In Windsor town there were
339 guest beds and stables for 669 horses.

The old Market House, being in 'a ruinous state', was pulled down, along with
the butchers' shambles next to it.

1687   *25th April* First establishment of a hackney coach stand on Castle Hill. No more than two coaches were allowed at a time.

Almshouses established at Pitt's Field (now known as Bachelors' Acre)
The building of the Guildhall begun by Sir Thomas Fitch.

The Builder of the Guildhall

Sir Thomas Fitch, who is often credited with the design of the best-known building in Windsor, the Guildhall, was not a Windsor man and does not appear to have had any other connection with the town. So little was known about him that he was not even included in the *Dictionary of National Biography* until they produced an extra volume of Missing Persons. He was born in Barkway, Hertfordshire, and initially worked as a bricklayer and then became a carpenter and building contractor. It was the rebuilding of the capital following the Great Fire of London in 1666 that made his name. Among the projects he undertook was the deepening and wharfing of the Fleet ditch for which he had to employ 200 men. He also worked in Portsmouth and Winchester, as a contractor with an architect, although he is known to have designed his own house. He was knighted in 1679 and created a baronet on 7th September 1688 just nine days before he died, leaving our Guildhall unfinished. Unfortunately, the Windsor record that could have told us about the relationship between Fitch and Sir Christopher Wren is unreadable. There is no doubt that he was the contractor on the project, but did he design the building too?

Pamela Marson

1688   At the end of this year the crisis over James II's Catholic faith led to his flight, and the accession of his daughter, the protestant Mary II and William III. James left Windsor for the last time on 17th November, and William reached it on 14th December.

1689   *18th February* £20 plus a shilling was spent on the ceremony for proclaiming the new monarchs.

1690   From this date Windsor's MPs were chosen not by the corporation but by those inhabitants paying 'scot and lot'. Most of the 300-400 electors were to prove open to bribery.
The Guildhall was completed by Sir Christopher Wren.

1691   The market cross, known as Sadler's Cross, at the junction of High Street and Peascod Street, was demolished, but the ancient custom of proclaiming a new monarch on this spot is still continued. The pillory also disappeared.

Windsor Guildhall in 2000

1693   The King granted the mayor and churchwardens a £50 annuity for the relief of the poor.

1694   When Queen Mary died of smallpox 1s 6d was paid for tolling the bell at her funeral.

1696   This year saw the beginnings of a proper water supply for Windsor and Eton when John Yarnold built a waterworks at Eton. The mains were made of wood.

1698   *Summer* Celia Fiennes visited Windsor which she wrote 'lookes well, the streets large the market house on stone pillars and large hall on the top'. Richard Topham, keeper of the records at the Tower of London, became MP and served until 1713. He was Lord of the Manor of Clewer Brocas and his home, Pilgrim Place in Peascod Street, was noted for its treasures. A burial ground was acquired by the Quakers between Kings Road and the Sheet Field. It was still in use in 1826-27.

1700   *30th July* Prince George, only surviving son of the future Queen Anne, died at Windsor of a 'violent Feaver with a Rash', just four days after his twelfth birthday was celebrated with fireworks.

1701   *24th May* William III granted an annuity of £50 to the borough as compensation for losses, including the right to gravel extraction, sustained as a result of the enclosure of more land in the Home Park.

      John Yarnold built his second waterworks, this time on Tangier Island. The cistern at St George's Chapel, which held 16,200 gallons, was filled weekly.

1702   *8th March* The customary bell-ringing announced the accession of Queen Anne. She continued to live in her small house on the south side of the castle. Western Cottage was built (still found near Bachelors' Acre) for her secretary.

1703   The inhabitants of the hamlet of Dedworth were brought to trial at the assizes at Wallingford for refusing to pay poor and church rates levied by the parish of New Windsor.

1705   *3rd November* 'Whereas there is a considerable number of Children in this Town and Parish of New Windsor, who have little or no education given them, through the Povertie of their Parents, 'Tis now agreed & resolved upon by the Chief Inhabitants…in setting up a Charity School for that purpose.' Queen Anne with £50 headed a list of subscribers who raised £201.19.6 to build, staff and equip a charity or free school for 70 poor children. The school was held at first in the church, but in 1725 a purpose-built school was opened.

A Great Architect

Sir Christopher Wren (1632-1723) knew the town of Windsor well. His father, also Christopher Wren, had been Dean of Windsor, as was his uncle Matthew; so the young Christopher spent his boyhood among the wonderful old buildings of the chapter and chapel as well as the castle. During the English revolution, Oliver Cromwell's men occupied Windsor Castle so that Dean Wren and his family had to leave. It is thought that the architect built himself a house in the town and he could have designed the Guildhall. Maybe this was why he was asked to take over the supervision of the building of the Guildhall when Sir Thomas Fitch died. There is a well-known story that he caused much dismay when he insisted that no central pillars were needed to support the upper chamber. It is said that finally, to pacify the councillors, he placed pillars which did not reach the ceiling. He was a brilliant engineer with experience of buildings with vast unsupported roofs, so there is probably some truth in the story.

Beryl Hedges

1705   A hoard of coins and a medieval lamp (possibly from the hermitage) was
        found on land belonging to the estate of St Leonard's. The coins dated back to
        the Iron Age.

1706   Queen Anne paid for a bridge over the Thames at Datchet to replace the
        ferry. No tolls were charged for using this bridge and not surprisingly it
        became more popular than the Windsor crossing where charges were made.
        Compensation of £55 was awarded, plus £20 a year to cover these losses to
        the borough.

1707   The statue of Queen Anne was added to the Guildhall.

1709   Johannes Kip's engravings of Windsor were published in *Britannia
        Illustrata*.

1711   *July* Jonathan Swift lodged in Windsor Castle, hoping to obtain the Queen's
        favour and a deanery. He took a dislike to the town, calling it 'scoundrel'.

        A new ring of bells was hung in the parish church. They were made by
        Richard Phelps of the Whitechapel foundry and given by Samuel Masham,
        cofferer to Queen Anne.

1712   EJ Sargeant & Son, funeral directors, was founded in Slough.

1714   A messenger was sent to London with news of Queen Anne's death.
        George I was proclaimed with drums and trumpet.

1715   The Whig dominated House of Commons reversed Windsor's election of Tory
        MPs, one of whom was Christopher Wren, son of the architect, on the
        grounds of bribery.

1718   A butcher's shop next to the Guildhall was pulled down by its owner, Silas
        Bradbury, and as the foundations were dug for a new building the work was
        stopped by order of the mayor. He claimed the land belonged to the
        corporation and fenced the area off. A lawyer, called in to settle the dispute,
        found in favour of Bradbury. But the house that was built on the tiny site was
        too tall and as a result it now leans away from the Guildhall. The legend is that
        it does so in memory of that old quarrel. As Market Cross House this is now
        one of Windsor's most famous buildings.

1722   20 loads of timber were used to repair the bridge.

*Market Cross House
in 1998*

1724   *April* Thomas Randue, one of the founders of the proposed charity school, died, leaving £500 for the building of the school.

Avery Tyrrell of Windsor and Daniel Beaumont of Eton bought the waterworks for £300.

1725   *30th August* Accusations of extortion were levelled against Mr Beaumont. Subsequently the corporation gave a guinea towards the cost of a horse and cart so that Thomas Wikes could deliver water to the inhabitants of Windsor, while the method of supplying water was looked into.

The charity or free school building was completed in the north corner of the parish churchyard and the school opened there, with places for 40 boys and 30 girls (the school continued its existence in various forms until, as Princess Margaret Royal Free School, it was closed down in 2000).

1727   George II became king. Like his predecessor he took no interest in Windsor.

1728   Richard Topham bequeathed £500 for the building of a workhouse for the poor.

1730   *30th June* Complaints were made about the lack of water laid into the town and the consequent danger in the event of fire. The corporation decided to dispossess Mr Beaumont and to consider how water might better be supplied.

1731   Arabella Reeve, sister of Richard Topham, also left £500 for a workhouse.

1733   *31st November* An entry in the Quaker minute book for east Berkshire records that seven Friends attended a meeting at Windsor.

The workhouse was built where the pest house had been, with the proviso that if the plague returned it would revert to its former use.

Inspection of Windsor bridge revealed it to be again in a dangerous condition. Lord Sidney Beauclerk became MP and was to serve until 1744.

Four Arthurs

Today the name Vansittart means only a busy road, but for well over a century it was the surname of important local landowners.

The first **Arthur** (1691-1760) purchased the Manor of Clewer in 1718, having like his Dutch forebears made money from merchant adventuring. A year later he inherited the Manor of Shottesbrooke near White Waltham and chose to live there rather than at Clewer. **Arthur II** (1726-1806) led a wild youth as a member of the Hell Fire Club, and was a noted swordsman and duellist. But in respectable middle age he served as MP for Berkshire while maintaining his reputation for the exotic by keeping two elephants and a rhinoceros in Shottesbrooke Park. His nephew Nicholas (Lord Bexley, hence Bexley Street) was the most distinguished family member, becoming Chancellor of the Exchequer from 1812-1823. **Arthur III** (1775-1829), briefly MP for Windsor, had the land at Clewer surveyed prior to enclosure, and sold the manor house to the Foster family. The 6' 7" tall **Arthur IV** (1807-1859), soldier and gambler, won his bride after a race from London to Brighton; but nobody knew till his death he also kept a second family (the Stovells - and another road name). It was this Arthur whose sale of the Clewer land brought about Windsor's expansion westwards, so that the Vansittarts are remembered now only in the road which runs over the once-green acres of their former estate.

Hester Davenport with acknowledgements to Jean Kirkwood

Clock and Lock Makers

John Davis (1650-1713) was believed to be the son of a royal blacksmith in Windsor. He created the chiming clock in the Curfew Tower in 1689. His premises were in Thames Street. **John Davis II** (1690-1762) carried out much iron work for Eton College, including a clockwork roasting jack that was in use until 1920. He was most famous for his turret clocks installed in stately homes and churches all over southern England. Among them was the stable clock at Great Lodge, Windsor Park. In 1732 he took over responsibility for Windsor's waterworks. **John Davis III** (1722-1801) made several turret clocks including one for Bisham Abbey. He fitted a larger water wheel to the engine which pumped water to the top of the town, thus improving the service. In 1776 he received a Royal Warrant as 'Locksmith in Ordinary to His Majesty's Palace of Windsor Castle'. **George Davis** (1760-1833) invented a double-chambered lock which was adopted for Government despatch boxes. He declined the offer of a knighthood from King George III saying 'Sire, it would sound very odd, were I to meet a gentleman in the street, and he were to say "Sir George Davis, please to come and mend my smoke-jack"'. He became 'Locksmith and Ironmonger in Ordinary to King George IV'.

Hester Davenport with acknowledgements to Paul Ashworth

1736   *5th May* An act was passed making the mayor, bailiffs and burgesses responsible for Windsor bridge. They were allowed to keep the tolls but had to repair, maintain and rebuild it when necessary.

1737   The Countess of Hertford took up residence at a house called The Hermitage (later St Leonard's).

1738   *26th September* Visit by John Wesley who records in his journal that he 'declared the gospel of peace to a small company'. He was to preach in Windsor 14 times altogether.

At a parliamentary election Lord Vere Beauclerk and Richard Oldfield both polled 133 votes. The House of Commons declared in favour of Lord Vere Beauclerk.

1739   Great frost.

1741   *25th May* and *29th June* John Wesley preached in the town again.

1742   High Flood.
28th September An abortive attempt was made by rabble-rousers to prevent John Wesley preaching in the town.

William Collier's plan of the town and castle was published.

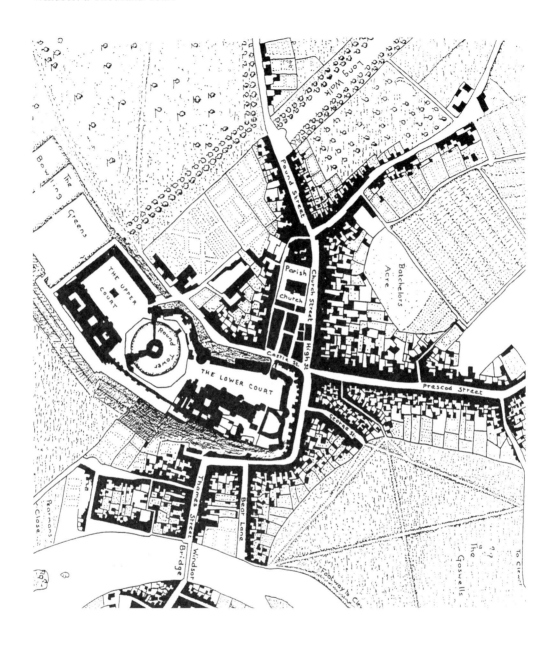

*Part of the map of Windsor Town and the Little Park made by William Collier in 1742
redrawn from the original*

1744   *11th June* Repairs to the Guildhall were found necessary and they were ordered to be carried out at a cost of not more that £40.

1745   *12th October* The mayor and members of the corporation attended a meeting at Reading to decide on measures to be taken in support of the King and his ministers against the Young Pretender (Bonnie Prince Charlie).

Joseph Pote produced a *Windsor and Eton Journal*, but it lasted only a few years.

1746   Horace Walpole rented a small house in the castle grounds. The neglected castle had been divided up into grace and favour apartments for elderly aristocratic ladies who passed their time in tea-drinking and card parties. The young Walpole enjoyed their tittle-tattle.

The first known advertisement for a stage coach from Windsor

WILL begin on Wednesday the 25th of this Inst. March, 1747, to set out from Mr. Smith's House in the Market-place in Windsor, every Morning at Six of the Clock, also the same Day, at Two in the Afternoon, and will go thro' Eton, Slough and Colnbrook, to the Bell-Savage Inn on Ludgate Hill in London; and will return from the said Bell-Savage Inn every Day at the same Hours, and will call at the Chequer-Inn at Charing Cross, where a regular Book is kept, and Places may be taken.
    Performed (if God permit) by *Benj. Smith* and *James Scotcher.*
    No Money, Plate, or Watches, will be answer'd for, unless entered and paid for accordingly.
N.B. Of the said *Benjamin Smith* and *James Scotcher*, may be had Hearses, Coaches, Landaus, Chariots, and Four-wheel'd Chaises; also Two-wheel Chaises in the nature of Post Chaises, to any part of Great-Britain.

1749   Joseph Pote published *The History and Antiquities of Windsor Castle.*

1750   *19th February* John Wesley preached in the town.
25th December Wesley recorded in his journal that he rode through a violent storm and preached to a 'little serious congregation' in Windsor.
St Leonard's was bought by Mr Lilley Aynscombe, who rebuilt it.

1752 A jewellery business was started at 9 Thames Street which was later taken over by Dysons.

Dr Samuel Johnson visited his friend Topham Beauclerk (grandson of Charles II and Nell Gwyn) at Pilgrim Place, which he had inherited.

1754 The Duke of Cumberland ('Butcher' Cumberland, who put down the 1745 Jacobite rebellion and is commemorated by the Obelisk in the Great Park) gave £350 to bribe the electorate to vote for Henry Fox and John Fitzwilliam, who were duly elected. Fox had caused a famous scandal by his secret marriage in 1744 to Lady Georgiana Lennox. Later created Baron Holland, he had first become a Windsor MP in 1741 and subsequently served for 20 years, holding important government offices.

1755 *3rd January* As the town gaol was too small the mayor and corporation decided to inspect it and consider how it could be enlarged.

Monthly meetings of Quakers in Windsor were abolished and united with the Reading meeting.

Joseph Pote published *Les Délices de Windsor, or a description of Windsor Castle* at 2 shillings for tourists, noting the many delightful houses of the nobility there and roundabout.

Painters of Windsor

Thomas and Paul Sandby came to Windsor from their childhood home in Nottingham. Thomas (1721-1798) showed early skill at perspective drawing and became a military draughtsman in the ordnance office at the Tower of London. He worked for William Augustus, Duke of Cumberland, at Culloden in 1746 and the Netherlands in 1747. When Cumberland became Ranger of Windsor Great Park, Sandby was appointed his deputy and was the architect responsible for many houses in Windsor, London and Cambridge, as well as the design of Virginia Water. He was first professor of architecture at the Royal Academy of Art. When he died in 1798 he was buried in Old Windsor churchyard. *The Gentleman's Magazine* said "By his decease the King has lost an honest and valuable servant, the neighbourhood of Windsor an inhabitant universally esteemed, and his family and friends one of the gentlest and best of human beings".

Like his older brother, Paul (1730-1809) started his career drawing for the Board of Ordnance - in fact he may have filled Thomas's place there while he was abroad. Paul spent much of his time between 1747 and 1752 making accurate drawings of the topography and scenery of the Highlands of Scotland. By 1760 he had several pupils and had produced many watercolours. He was, by this time, thought to be a better artist than his brother, with a particular gift for finely delineated figures and detail. He produced many views of Windsor. The Royal Collection contains a variety of work by both Sandby brothers including a number of pictures recorded as "Paul Sandby after Thomas Sandby" and other such mixed attributions. Though both were fine artists Thomas's work was more like an architect's drawing and where there is a greater feeling of realism with human interest the work is likely to be Paul's.

Margaret Gilson

1756   St Leonard's became the country retreat of William Pitt the Elder.

1758   Horace Walpole visited Richard Bateman's Chinese property at Old Windsor.
        Influenced by Walpole, Bateman later redesigned it in the Gothic style and
        called it The Priory. It attracted visitors for its many curiosities.

1760   *25th October* At the age of 22, George III
        succeeded his grandfather as king.

1761   A lease for Bachelors' Acre was granted to Christopher Lofft for 40 years, at
        3s 4d a year, with the proviso that it must remain open for 'any lawful
        recreation at all convenient times'. At about this time the group calling itself
        the Bachelors of Windsor was inaugurated.

        Admiral the Honourable Augustus Keppel, who had had a distinguished naval
        career and had sailed round the world with Anson, was elected MP. He was
        re-elected in 1765, 1768 and 1774, and regarded himself as acting for the
        town against the crown.

1764   High floods lasted on and off for 15 weeks.

1766   There was a great frost and the water works were frozen.

1767   *5th October* Thomas Rutter was fined for refusing to accept the office of
        mayor and sending a 'very contemptuous message' to that effect to the
        corporation.

1768   High floods.
        The inhabitants petitioned for a bill for the paving, lighting and cleaning of the
        streets.

1769   *30th March* An Act of Parliament was passed vesting responsibility for the
        state of the streets in a body of 61 commissioners. They could order the
        paving of streets, making of drains and the erection of lamps.

1769   A night constable and six watchmen were appointed. They had the power to arrest vagrants and disorderly persons, and were known as Charlies. George III contributed £1,000 towards a public subscription to effect these improvements.
Lord Charles Spencer, the Hon. Aubrey Beauclerk and Arthur Vansittart were given the freedom of the borough for their services in preventing the infringement of the corporation's rights in the paving, lighting and cleaning bill.

1770   A chemist's shop opened at 50 High Street and Roberts Windsor Soap was first sold there. The shop is no longer a chemist but it still sells soap under the name of Woods of Windsor.

Squire of Windsor

King George III loved Windsor and was popular with Windsorians, knowing many by name and showing a good-natured interest in their affairs. He was a great hunter, and local inns filled up on hunting days. He was also deeply interested in farming, earning the nickname 'Farmer George'. He visited his farm labourers in their cottages, always leaving something behind for the poorest. He established a custom of 'terracing' on the South Terrace, on summer evenings parading there with his family, chatting to all and sundry. He also encouraged Windsor children to play cricket or fly their kites in the Park. With Queen Charlotte the King patronised local shops. Charles Knight tells how he was once found in his father's bookshop calmly reading Thomas Paine's anti-monarchist *The Rights of Man*. He gave generously to the town for road improvements, for a soldiers' hospital, and for establishing the Theatre Royal. Less creditably he paid large sums to get his own man elected Windsor's MP.

In November 1788, at the time of his first 'madness', Windsor citizens watched in distress as he left for the greater privacy of Kew. On his recovery and return in March 1789 the town rejoiced, paying £40 for a firework display from the Round Tower. His Golden Jubilee in 1810 was another celebration, but sadly the King was too ill to attend. From then until his death in 1820 he lived in a permanent state of derangement in the sunless rooms overlooking the North Terrace.

Hester Davenport

1771   *31st July* The bridge was found to be in such a poor condition that carts and coaches going over it were in danger of falling through. Immediate repairs were ordered.

Lady Maria Waldegrave, who owned St Leonard's Hill, commissioned Thomas Sandby to build additions to it, and she called it Forest Lodge.

1772   To the King's annoyance his brother William, Duke of Gloucester, married the widowed Lady Waldegrave (she started life as the illegitimate daughter of a milliner). Forest Lodge became Gloucester Lodge. The Duke bought St Leonard's and called it Sophia Farm after his daughter, Princess Sophia.

1773   A new workhouse was erected in Sheet Street with money given by Samuel Travers, who had been Windsor MP and surveyor-general to William III.

1774   Disastrous floods occurred and as a result the streets had to be re-paved.

1776   Queen Anne's house was given to Queen Charlotte and rebuilt to house the large royal family because the castle was uninhabitable. The house was known as Queen's Lodge, and was at the top of the Long Walk. The public road to Old Windsor and Staines passed between it and the castle.

1777   A soldier from the barracks preached at the 'hole in the wall', a cottage in Sun Passage, later said to be the cradle of Windsor congregationalism.

1778   George III took up residence in Queen's Lodge, and became the town's chief patron.

1779   Richard Martin became innkeeper of the Castle Inn (formerly known as the Mermaid Inn). He remained as innkeeper for over a decade, during which time he was the Windsor postmaster and holder of a Royal warrant to provide extra horses and carriages for George III as required.

1780   After a plentiful distribution of bribes, the King's candidate, Penyston Portlock Powney, defeated Admiral Keppel in the election by 16 votes.
A riot between the townspeople and a regiment of militia, the Lancashire Volunteers, had to be put down by a troop of cavalry.

1781   St Leonard's (formerly Sophia Farm) was sold by the Duke of Gloucester to Mr G. Birch.

1782   St Leonard's Hill was bought by William, later 3rd Earl Harcourt.
He was a successful military commander, and Deputy Ranger of Windsor Great Park.

1783   *26th November* George III watched a small balloon being filled with hydrogen gas by Professor Argand. It floated away over Windsor fields.

1784   A hospital for sick soldiers was built on a piece of land, called Glaziers Corner, situated at the left side of the Long Walk about a mile from the town, after Colonel Trigg of the twelfth regiment, then on duty at Windsor, had petitioned the King. It was converted to labourers' cottages in 1812.

1785   *31st March* Charles Knight Senior published the first Windsor Guide. This book and its revisions remained the standard guide to the town for 40 years. Beaumont Lodge at Old Windsor was rebuilt in the classical style for Henry Griffiths.

The King's Astronomer

The famous astronomer, **Sir William Herschel**, and his sister Caroline had a brief association with Old Windsor from June 1785 to April 1786, when they rented Clayhall Farm house from Mrs Keppel, daughter of the late Sir Edward Walpole. William Herschel had sprung to international fame when, on 13th March 1781, he discovered the planet Uranus, the first new planet to be discovered since the dawn of history. In August 1782 King George III offered him a post as King's Astronomer, and the family moved to Datchet so as to be near Windsor Castle and in 1783 he built his large 20-foot telescope. Two years later when he was making plans to build an even greater, 40-foot telescope, for which the King had made him a grant of £2000, a severe illness made it essential that they should move. Clayhall seemed to present an ideal situation, on the edge of the Great Park, with a clear horizon, and more convenient to the castle than Datchet. Sadly it was a great disappointment. As Caroline recorded: '... when my brother was going to lay the foundations for the 40-foot, he found that he had to deal with a litigious woman who told him he must expect to have his rent raised each year, according to the improvements he was making on the premises; on which he thought it advisable to look for another suitable spot...'. On 3rd April 1786 the Herschels moved to what later became known as Observatory House in Slough where they remained until William's death in 1822. The house stood until 1969, when it was pulled down by the Crown Commissioners - probably unaware of its historical connections.

AE Fanning

December The novelist and diarist Fanny Burney visited the elderly Mrs Mary Delany at the home in St Albans Street provided for her by the King and Queen. 1786-1791 mark the years of Fanny's service as a Keeper of the Robes, mainly spent in Windsor.

1786   Warren Hastings, former governor general of India, bought Beaumont, a 91 acre estate at Old Windsor, for £12,000, where he lived until 1791. Behind the classical portico guests found an Indianised environment, with Indian servants, paintings and porcelain, the air scented with attar of roses.

1788   *30th November* From the autumn the King had become increasingly ill with his so-called 'madness' and it was decided to move him to Kew for greater privacy. As described by Fanny Burney 'almost all Windsor was collected round the rails to witness the mournful spectacle of his departure, which left them in the deepest despondence'

A Milliner's shop in Windsor, by SW Fores, 1787, showing King George III, Queen Charlotte
and a princess examining the goods.
© *The British Museum*

1789   *19th March* The King was well enough to return and this time Fanny wrote
       that 'everything and everybody were smiling and lively. All Windsor came out
       to meet the king. It was a joy amounting to extacy'. The town contributed 40
       guineas for a display of fireworks from the Round Tower that evening.

       Henry Griffiths bought more property in Old Windsor including the area
       known as Lyon's Green, near the Bells of Ouseley where many of the
       villagers lived. In order to improve his view of the river, he evicted his tenants
       and demolished their houses but did provide alternative accommodation.

1790   The first road map to show Windsor was published. Such 'strip' maps, which
       follow the lengths of roads rather than the contours of the land, are now
       collectors' items.

1791   Charles Knight was born. He lived with his widowed father, also Charles
       Knight, who kept a bookshop and was mayor of Windsor in 1806 and 1817.

1792   *July* Dorothy Wordsworth stayed with her uncle and aunt in the Horseshoe
        Cloisters and attended Egham Raceball at the Guildhall.

1793   A Theatre Royal was built in the High Street and frequently attended by the
        King and Queen. It was so small that His Majesty's apothecary in the lower
        boxes claimed he might have felt his pulse across the pit. Performances were
        only allowed during Eton College vacations.

1794   Romney Lock was first built.
        In the elections for MPs this year only 29 of 320 electors were prepared to
        state that they had not received a bribe.

1795   Construction of the infantry barracks began (completed 1803). The site was
        an acre of land in Sheet Street next to the workhouse. Initially it housed 750
        soldiers and eventually 1000 men. In 1799 the first occupants were the First
        Regiment of Foot Guards, Grenadier Guards.

        Windsor Volunteers was founded, it was the Home Guard of the day.

1797   Romney Lock was opened. Cutlers Ait and the Cobbler were extended
        upstream.
        Foundation of Penny Royal Almshouses at Old Windsor.

1798   Death of Thomas Sandby, artist and architect, who was buried at Old Windsor.

1799   As a child actor with a band of strolling players Edmund Kean performed
        Tom Thumb at one of Windsor's three annual fairs.

Pennyroyal Cottages - the Almshouses, Old Windsor.   M. F. Gilson

1800   Construction of cavalry barracks began (completed 1804). They were built on 14 acres of land on the Spital Road (St Leonard's Road), to house 424 cavalry soldiers and their horses. It also included two hospitals, one for the cavalry and one for the infantry. The first occupants were the 13th Dragoons, who only stayed two months.
Knight's Bookshop moved to 2 Castle Hill.

1801   *10th, 11th, 12th May*   An old ceremony, the perambulation of the parish of New Windsor, was revived. The mayor led a cheerful 3-day procession which marked boundary trees and stopped at boundary houses to sing psalms, eat rolls and butter and drink wine. In between these points they forded streams, climbed over walls and through hedges. Where the boundary ran through water (at the 'Pickell Herring Ponds') swimmers were employed. On the first day, in fine spring weather, the troop set off downhill from the Guildhall, crossed the stinking Goswell ditches on planks, then moved on to Datchet Bridge and Old Windsor Green, winding up at Frogmore House where Queen Charlotte provided roast beef and plum pudding. After two more days the jollifications concluded with the broaching of a barrel of Windsor ale at the Guildhall.

St Andrew's Church Clewer, at the beginning of the nineteenth century.

1801 cont.   *Autumn* The price of bread had risen during the war with France, causing great hardship among the poor. Protesters broke bakers' windows in the High Street.

Windsor Bank and Windsor and Eton Bank were both founded this year.

20th December Death of Mary 'Perdita' Robinson, writer and former mistress of George, Prince of Wales. She was buried in Old Windsor churchyard.

Perdita's Tomb in Old Windsor Churchyard

1802   *April* The conclusion of a peace with Napoleon was celebrated with a series of illuminations, transparent coloured designs lit from behind depicting patriotic figures.

John Williams was unseated as MP for Windsor for bribery.

1803   A master was appointed to teach the choristers of St George's Chapel reading, writing, arithmetic and their duty to God and Man. This is the first time that the education of choristers was separated from the music.

August War with France had broken out again and, fearful of invasion, the Windsor Volunteers drilled in the park and learned to handle a musket.

1804   *22nd October* The Royal Regiment of Horse Guards, the Blues, moved into the Cavalry barracks and remained there until February 1821. After this they returned every three years for one year, alternating with the two regiments of Life Guards.

1805   Warren Hastings sold his house at Old Windsor to Lord Ashbrook for £13,939.

1806   From this year until 1831 there was no contest at elections, an agreement having been made that one candidate would be put forward by the castle another by the borough.

Windsor Forest Act was passed appointing commissioners to enquire into the boundaries of the Forest and the Crown land within it.

William Wordsworth visited his uncle in Horseshoe Cloisters, having previously been banned from Windsor for his sympathy for the French Revolution.

Mary, the future Countess of Harcourt, established a charity school at Clewer Green. It was known as Harcourt Charity School (later Clewer Green School).

The cottages where the Harcourt Charity School was established

1807   The theatre in the High Street was purchased as a meeting room for the independents (later known as the Congregationalists) who since 1781 had been meeting first in Goswell Lane and then in Bier Lane.

1809   Disastrous floods.

1810   *25th October* The Golden Jubilee of George III was celebrated by the
        Bachelors of Windsor on Bachelors' Acre with an ox roast and plum
        puddings. The King himself was too ill to attend, but the mayor and
        corporation greeted Queen Charlotte, the Duke of York and other princes and
        princesses, serving them with slices of the meat on silver dishes. In the
        evening there was an illuminated water pageant. There was also a ball at the
        Guildhall, at which a silk rope separated the attorneys' wives and daughters
        from the grocers' wives and daughters.
        2nd November The death of the King's favourite daughter, Princess Amelia,
        at her sister's house in St Albans Street, precipitated an irreversible insanity.

1811   *19th May* An obelisk was erected on Bachelors' Acre to commemorate the
        previous year's Golden Jubilee festivities. These festivities were held annually
        on the acre until 1855.

1812   *1st August* The first edition of the *Windsor and Eton Express* was published
        by the Charles Knights, father and son. The newspaper is still published.
        Darvilles started trading in the town as grocers.

Newspaper Pioneer

Charles Knight (1791-1873), writer, publisher and philanthropist, was one of Windsor's most distinguished citizens. The son of another Charles Knight who kept a bookshop at 2 Castle Hill, his childhood memories published in *Passages of a Working Life* (1864) paint a vivid picture of the town of his boyhood, contrasting the comings and goings of royalty with the problems of poverty and insanitariness then. On 1st August 1812, when the Napoleonic Wars had made newspaper tax high, the two Knights bravely started a weekly newspaper, The *Windsor and Eton Express*. Despite the price (seven old pence), it proved  successful and the younger man continued as editor until 1827, after which he made his name as a book publisher.

Charles Knight was a man of social conscience who believed passionately that good quality reading matter should be available to all, not just the better off. He was placed in charge of publications for the SDUK (Society for the Diffusion of Useful Knowledge, founded 1826). For them, in 1832, he launched *The Penny Magazine*, a well-written, well illustrated weekly, priced within reach of all but the poorest. Many working men passed it one to another. Knight's vision and enterprise led to many other series, including the *Pictorial Bible, Pictorial Shakespeare*, and a *Library for the Young*. When he died (at Addlestone) in 1873 his body was brought back to Windsor for burial in Bachelor's Acre, where gates erected in his memory can still be seen. A plaque marks his grave.

Hester Davenport

The Advertisement

From SUNDAY, OCTOBER 3, *to* SUNDAY, OCTOBER 10, 1813.

M. CALEY,
Milliner, Dress-Maker, and Haberdasher,
LATE OF THAMES-STREET, WINDSOR,

BEGS Leave to inform the Ladies of Windsor, Eton, and their Environs; that the above Business will in future be carried on in Castle-Street, in conjunction with her Sister, Mrs. NOKE.

M. C. takes this Opportunity of returning her most grateful Thanks for the numerous and distinguished Favors hitherto so liberally conferred; and (jointly with her Sister) most respectfully solicits a Continuance of the same.

1813   'Mrs' Maria Caley, milliner to Queen Charlotte, opened her first shop by the castle ditch.

Windsor Forest Inclosure Act was passed. Windsor Forest ceased to exist as a legal entity and land was allotted in lieu of forest rights including the right of deer to graze anywhere within it.

The discovery of the coffin of Charles I, the severed head still with pointed beard, made sensational news for the *Windsor Express*.
19th December The poet Shelley briefly rented a Windsor house for himself and his first wife, Harriet.

1814   Great frost. Shallow wells became polluted by cesspools and river pollution too had become very serious.

The meeting house in High Street was enlarged and became known as the Chapel of the Dissenters.

Following the abdication of Napoleon and his exile on Elba, the Duke of Wellington was greeted enthusiastically on a visit to Windsor to review a regiment of horse guards (the Blues). His horses were removed from his carriage and it was pulled to the Castle Inn where a reception was held in his honour.

1815   *30th April* After Napoleon's escape from Elba the Blues marched from Windsor, embarking for Belgium and ultimately the field of Waterloo. News of the victory on 18th June was brought to Windsor by a courier. On their return the surviving soldiers were feted with a dinner laid out on tables in the Long Walk.

September Shelley, Mary Godwin (later his second wife) and Thomas Love Peacock set off from the Bells of Ouseley to row up the Thames to Lechlade and back.

A new theatre, accommodating 500, was opened in Thames Street.

1816   A Wesleyan Methodist chapel was built in Bier Lane.

Two of the three banks in Windsor failed - Windsor Bank and Windsor and Eton Bank.

1817   Queen Charlotte attended the public meeting held to promote the establishment of a free dispensary.

Clewer Inclosure Act was passed. The village greens at Clewer and Dedworth were divided and the ancient open fields with their common rights soon ceased to exist. The landscape was transformed, but villagers living around Clewer and Dedworth Greens were compensated for their loss of rights under enclosure. The Fuel Allotments Award instructed the rector, churchwardens and overseer of the poor to hold land in trust to supply turves, ferns and other fuel to occupiers of houses valued at not more than £5 a year.

Bachelors' Acre became the property of the corporation.

19th November Disorder and drunken undertakers marred the funeral of Princess Charlotte, the Prince Regent's daughter, who had died in childbirth. The memorial statue by Matthew Wyatt in St George's Chapel was paid for by public subscription, with contributions limited to one shilling per person.

1818   Maria Caley was awarded a Royal Warrant as milliner.

The free dispensary supported by Queen Charlotte was established in Church Street by Edward Locker for the 'relief of the sick poor of Windsor, Eton and the vicinity'. The Queen died at the end of the year.

In the Prince Regent's desire for privacy the public road to Old Windsor under the south terrace was diverted further from the castle.

1820   *29 January* Death of George III. Shops closed, and despite the long years of his separation from public life even the poor wore tokens of sympathy.
16 February Thirty thousand flocked to Windsor for the old king's torch-lit funeral in St George's Chapel. A procession of black clad mourners accompanied the funeral-car to the sound of muffled drums, trumpets, the firing of minute guns and the tolling of the bell.

The National School, for children of Established Church families, was set up in Peascod Street.

The parish church was found to be unsafe and it was decided to demolish it and build a new one.

The New Road (Victoria Street and Clarence Road) was created, allowing for new house building. Materials from the destruction of Queen's Lodge were used.

The last salmon was caught at Windsor until the late twentieth century.

1821   Disastrous floods.

1822   *24th June* The new parish church, designed by Charles Hollis, was consecrated by the Bishop of Salisbury, the Rt Rev. John Fisher.

10th July The first stone of new Windsor bridge was laid by Frederick Duke of York, George IV's brother. The engineer was Thomas Telford and the architect Charles Hollis.

1823   *June* Work began to carry out the reconstruction of the castle by Sir Jeffrey Wyattville, whose alterations were to alter the appearance of the castle and therefore the views of the town for ever. He also developed Royal Lodge, where George IV preferred to live.

4th August The King closed the south terrace of the castle to the public except for Sundays. This was unpopular with Windsorians but the extension of the Long Walk to the new George IV Gate was widely welcomed.

Maria Caley moved her flourishing milliner's shop to premises opposite the Guildhall, where today's Caleys stands.

The Thames was frozen solid at Old Windsor.

1824   The building of the new bridge was completed. It is a cast iron structure of 3 spans with granite-faced piers

This view of the Round Tower was published in
The Windsor Guide 1793 by Charles Knight (senior).
It is considered to be the most accurate drawing
of the tower before it was altered in the late 1820s
and early 1830s by Sir Jeffrey Wyatville.
The skyline was changed for ever.

1826   William Riley of Forest Lodge in Winkfield Road had built a large house in Hermitage Lane which was divided into a Roman Catholic chapel and accommodation for the priest. It was registered as a Roman Catholic chapel. William thus fulfilled the dying wish of his father, John. When St Edward's Church was built, the house and chapel were sold and divided into two houses, the Old Hermitage and the Hermitage.

1827   A meeting was held at the Castle Hotel, arranged by the vicar, Isaac Gosset, to discuss the provision of gas in the town. The Windsor Royal Gaslight Company was founded following two years of trials in the area.

1828   The supply of gas was introduced to the town, the 'greatest improvement for centuries' according to the *Windsor Express*. The works were sited in Goswell meadow and the gas was made from wood and resin.

1829   The Metropolitan Police were established and their duties extended to royal palaces, including Windsor Castle, but not to the Great Park or the town.

        Thomas Bedborough, builder and property developer, added the red brick annex to the Guildhall.

Noble Benefactors

Third Earl, Field-Marshall William Harcourt was born in 1743 and inherited the title from his brother, George Simon, who died without children. William had a distinguished military career serving under the Duke of York in Flanders. He was given command of the army when the Duke returned home. The Earl and his wife, **Mary**, were on intimate terms with the royal family, William being present in the period of George III's illness and Mary acting as Queen Charlotte's confidante. In 1782 the Earl purchased St Leonard's Hill Estate and the Harcourts became generous benefactors, particularly to the parish of Clewer. The Clewer Green School was formerly known at the Harcourts' Charity as the Countess had left £500 in her will for the benefit of the Clewer Parish. The Earl was the first president of the dispensary and his wife left it £500 in her will. The Earl died in June 1830 at St Leonard's Hill, aged 87, and as he had no children the title became extinct. The Countess died in 1833 and both were buried at Stanton Harcourt. The Harcourt memorial tablet can be found in Clewer Church and also a notice recording an extract from the will of the Countess is attached to the wall of the bell tower.

Sheila Rooney

1829   The Oxford Blue public house, converted from two game-keepers' cottages,

was opened at Old Windsor by Thomas Evans, a Water-
loo veteran. During the battle he had shown conspicuous
bravery by rescuing his Colonel after killing four
cuirassiers and breaking his sword on a fifth. The pub
was named after his regiment in the horse guards, the
Blues. When a troop of the Blues and the Royals passes
the inn today, the order is given 'Eyes Left'.

Picture, courtesy of the Oxford Blue Inn,
shows a Trooper in the uniform at the time of Waterloo.

1830   The accession of William IV.
Coal was used to make gas as resin had proved unreliable.
William, 3rd Earl Harcourt of St Leonard's Hill, died. His statue can be seen
in St George's Chapel.

1831   *3rd September* Mr and Mrs Graham used the town gas supply to fuel a
balloon ascent from the Upper Mews. Though crowds flocked to see it, Mr
Graham lost money as few were willing to pay to enter the mews itself to
watch the initial ascent.
A huge equestrian statue of King George III by Sir Richard Westmacott was
completed at the end of the Long Walk on Snow Hill. It is popularly known as
the Copper Horse.

1832   A Congregational Chapel was started in William Street, the builder being
Jesse Hollis.
A turnpike road was built from Windsor to Dedworth, part of the new route to
Twyford and the Bath Road. This road is now Clarence Road and Dedworth
Road.
The part of Clewer which lay within the town and was known as Clewer
Within, was taken into the parliamentary borough under the Reform Act. But
voting was still open and corruption continued.

1833   *30th April* The Congregational Chapel in William Street opened.
Water supply was still unsatisfactory and a meeting was held at the Guildhall
to complain and to demand its improvement.
Pigs were still a problem too: Mr Jones, pork butcher, was prosecuted for
dumping filth in the street and Mr Davis for allowing his pigs to wander.

Countess Harcourt of St Leonard's Hill died and the Marquise d'Harcourt
moved into the house. In her will the Countess left £500 to be invested to
purchase clothing for distribution each Christmas to the eight poorest widows
of Clewer.

1834   The dispensary moved to a new building by Bachelors' Acre.

1835   The Municipal Reform Act was passed by parliament. It abolished the old
town council, replacing it by elected councilors. The first municipal elections
were held on 31st December. Ten Liberals and eight Tories were returned.
Six aldermen were elected by the new council.

Work started on the building of the union workhouse at Old Windsor, on land
donated by William IV.

THE UNION WORKHOUSE.   M.F Gilson

Richard Oxley became sole proprietor of the *Windsor Express*, which
remained under the control of the Oxley family at their printing works off
Bachelors' Acre until the 1970s.

1836   *June* Windsor's first fire brigade was formed after a fire destroyed 110 Thames Street, killing three of its occupants.

        22nd September The foundation stone of a new Wesleyan Methodist Chapel off Peascod Street was laid.

        Windsor Borough Police formed. The Borough Treasurer paid for uniforms and wages from March.

        Windsor and Eton Choral Society first met at the home of George Job Elvey, organist at St George's Chapel.

1837   *June* The second Wesleyan Methodist Chapel in Windsor opened off Peascod Street (on the site of the present King Edward Court Entrance).

        Nevile Reid & Co. purchased the Windsor Brewery of Ramsbottom and Legh, and most of its tied houses.

Slums and Steam Trains

Victoria came to the throne in June in 1837 after the death of her uncle, William IV. She was eighteen years old and destined to reign for sixty-three years and seven months, ruling over the largest empire the world has ever known, numbering her subjects in the hundreds of millions. The Victorian Age named after her long reign is synonymous with certain values, which chime with the aspirations at the height of the British Empire's power and wealth. The industrial revolution had contributed to this wealth but in Windsor the impact was slow to arrive.

Windsor remained a small market town with an ancient castle and a resident garrison. The expensive reconstruction of the castle, which had begun in the reign of George IV was just completed as Victoria came to the throne. She made it her principal residence and used it frequently to entertain other Royal Heads of State. The presence of the court brought employment to the town and also more tourists, a trend which increased relentlessly and shows no sign of abating even in the 21st century.

But if we take a look at the town behind the grandeur of the court a different picture emerges. Described by Jonathan Swift in the 18th century as 'Scoundrel', by the time Victoria came to the throne the dirtiness and overcrowding of the town had grown much worse. The road known as Bier Lane - supposedly named thus because of the practice of carrying corpses down to the river for despatch to the burial ground at Clewer - had degenerated to a warren of mean buildings, utterly lacking in any form of sanitation with backyard refuse heaps draining through the houses when the river flooded.

The general impression which assailed the visitor was one of squalor. It was described in detail in a report by Edward Cresy, Superintendent Inspector of the Board of Health in 1838, who reported on the open cesspools, the garbage heaps and the sewage which stagnated in the ditches and the smells and overcrowding which led inevitably to disease and death. Of every hundred children born, fifteen died in their first year, thirty-two before they were five and forty-two before they were fifteen.

From the local paper, the *Windsor Express*, we catch other glimpses of the seedier side of Windsor. There are references, for example, to the 'gaming and other disorderly houses' and to a meeting held at the Guildhall for the purpose of taking into consideration the most prompt means of suppressing the practice of gambling, which had reached unprecedented heights in the town. Streets 'swarmed with prostitutes and beggars'.

Windsor was a garrison town and with its abundant beer shops it is hardly surprising that intemperance and violence were part of life in the overcrowded and degrading slums. It was the plight of the destitute 'fallen women' that moved Mariquita Tennant to found the House of Mercy which grew into the Anglican Convent of St John the Baptist in Clewer under the outstanding leadership of its foundress, Harriet Monsell.

The situation began to improve with the passing of the Public Health Act in 1848, although a certain apathy assailed the corporation when the matter of the state of the town drains needed some resolution. Their attitude could be read in the statement which frequently followed any discussion for improvements: 'unnecessarily extravagant and infinitely beyond the means of the inhabitants'.

The town council, however, was enthusiastically diligent about loyal addresses to visiting royalty. Between 1852 and 1874 the mayor and corporation welcomed no less than eleven royal visitors including Napoleon III and Empress Eugenie, the Shah of Persia and the Tsar of all the Russias. Decorative arches for the carriages to pass under were a feature of this period and the corporation encouraged the townsfolk to decorate the houses and streets. Lavish illuminations were all part of the show and gas lighting and oil lamps were lit in abundance: the fire precautions did not seem to be a priority. When the Prince of Wales brought his prospective bride, Princess Alexandra of Denmark, to Windsor in 1863, the rain fell continuously but a great crowd welcomed her. The inevitable triumphal arch was erected in Thames Street but the mayor, already soaked, wisely decided not to read out the loyal address. Instead he threw it into the carriage thus foregoing his coveted opportunity to speak to a Royal Princess.

By the middle of the 19th century Windsor ceased to be a small, sleepy country town, as the advent of the railways increased its lure as a tourist attraction and brought it within reach of a larger, more mobile public. The council, having shown very little reforming zeal in its apathetic efforts to clean up the town, was galvanised into action on the matter of the railway and the opposition to it by both Eton College and the Crown. Dr Hawtrey, the headmaster of Eton College, protested that ' the boys would use the railway to travel up to London for 'vice' and would throw stones at the trains'. The Crown was unhappy about many aspects, even the effect of the smoke on its newly furbished walls. By the end of 1849 Windsor had obtained two branch lines and two railway stations, one on Riverside and one under the walls of the castle, the outcome of one of the bitterest conflicts in railway history - a story of rivalry, antagonism, prejudice and vested interests.

The money which the rival railway companies were prepared to invest resulted in the clearances of some of the terrible slums, particularly those which clustered under the walls of the castle. Trade, particularly the transport of goods by rail instead of the river enriched the tradesmen. With rising prosperity went the building of new homes such as those in the districts of Gloucester Place for the middle classes and Bexley Street for the respectable labouring class. However, the housing for the poor was still unsatisfactory except for the Prince Consort Cottages which were intended as a model of responsible house building. The new housing and roads gave Windsor its present Victorian look and with the arrival of the railway with its fast access to London, Windsor became a suburban town.

The Victorian era was a religious, church-going period and the town reflected this as two new parishes were created along with eight new places of worship. These were in addition to the parish church of St John, the Congregational Chapel in William Street and the Wesleyan Chapel in Peascod Street. At Holy Trinity, the garrison church, soldiers marched to church parade every Sunday. The Catholics built St Edward's for the increasing Catholic population and the many RC soldiers, to replace the small chapel at the Hermitage in Hermitage Lane. Much of education was in the hands of the churches and there are a bewildering number of schools mentioned in the records of the period. Some lasted only a few years or merged with other schools so it is confusing to try to follow the history of individual schools. Although Eton remains the most famous of the schools in the area, other reputable schools can trace their foundation to this period.

Services such as gas and water were still in the hands of private enterprise but at the first quarter of the century the *Windsor Express* comments 'As respects the improvement of the town generally the introduction of gas is decidedly the greatest which has been known for centuries'. The quality of drinking water available to the people was of a questionable standard. The waterworks was situated in Eton and medical men urged the corporation to effect some improvement in the standard of the town's water supply, but it was too late to prevent outbreaks of waterborne diseases such as cholera and typhoid in 19th century Windsor, the most famous casualty being the Prince Consort himself.

There was no organised police force at the beginning of Victoria's reign. There was a night constable and six watchmen who had power to arrest vagrants and disorderly persons but this was inadequate protection for an increasing population. With the passing of the Municipal Reform Act in 1835 the police force became the responsibility of the council. The Charity Commissioners allowed the old workhouse in Sheet Street to be sold to the council for use as a police station and lock-up.

All was not doom and gloom in Windsor throughout this period. The arts flourished under the patronage of the Royal family. The Queen was responsible for the foundation of the Royal Albert Institute in memory of the Prince Consort, which was founded to promote the study of literature, science and the fine arts. The children of the Sovereign, especially

Princesses Helena, Louise and Beatrice and Prince Leopold, all supported and encouraged interest in music and the arts. The century saw the foundation of many such societies and the growing interest in sport also led to several sports clubs being founded.

The town of Windsor has a story of its own which is often overshadowed by the proximity of the castle. Its destiny lies in the hands of those whom it elects as representatives on the town council but the developing power of the council during the 19th century was not matched by an understanding of its responsibilities. Windsor's representation in Parliament was reduced from two members to one member in 1868, and in the election of 1870 a conservative won the seat after many years of the liberals being in power.

The greatest gift that Queen Victoria gave to the people of Windsor was her encouragement of her husband's interest in the welfare of the town. If Albert had lived longer his legacy would have been greater and it is a sad irony that it was probably a strain of the lethal bacteria which was endemic in the town that caused his death; the town which he tried so hard to help.

Sheila Rooney

1837   *19th June*   King William IV died at the castle. The public was admitted to the lying-in-state in the Waterloo Chamber.
The mayor of Windsor, Edward Bovingdon, invited neighbouring gentry and local inhabitants of Windsor to assemble at the town hall to hear Victoria proclaimed Queen.

22nd June   Opening of Wesleyan Methodist Chapel, off Peascod Street.

10th July   At a special meeting the town council expressed its condolences to the new Queen on the death of her uncle and to the Dowager Queen Adelaide. A loyal address which congratulated the Queen on her accession was prepared.
22nd August   Queen Victoria arrived in Windsor amid scenes of rejoicing.
23rd August   The Bachelors of Windsor, accompanied by the Windsor and Eton junior cricket team, formed a procession at the Swan Inn and marched through the town where they took up their positions on either side of the Long Walk where a triumphal arch had been erected. The Queen drove through the arch on her way to the town. A public dinner was provided for the poor of the town in the Long Walk. Mrs Graham, the balloonist, made a successful ascent but was forced down by heavy rain at Stanwell.
24th August   A public dinner and ball was held at the Guildhall.
15th September   Windsor and Eton Royal Horticultural Society met in the grounds of the home of Captain Bulkeley at Spital.

1838   *15th August* The first meeting of Windsor's Baptist Church.
The Grenadier Guards was the first regiment to use the railway from Slough to London, to get to Queen Victoria's coronation. Before the coming of the railway it took a regiment two days to march to London, staying overnight at Staines, Colnbrook or Hounslow.

1839   Clewer House School had opened by this time. The first head was William Redford Harris. This was a private school of great distinction.
A bakery was set up in Oxford Road, which lasted until 1992, when it was known as Duffy's.
May The foundation stone of the Baptist Church in Victoria Street was laid.
16th October The Baptist Church was opened.
Stephen Hawtrey formed a choir of boys from the National School to sing for the services at Dedworth. When he went to Holy Trinity Church, Hawtrey took the choir with him. In 1846 he opened St. Mark's School where music lessons were held during school hours.
St Anne's School (later renamed Holy Trinity School) founded.

1840   *10th February* Queen Victoria and Prince Albert of Saxe-Coburg arrived in Windsor following their marriage. The town was decorated with gas and oil illuminations and the walls of the houses glowed with crowns and stars.
10th February Charles Dickens visited Windsor with his friends Daniel Maclise and John Forster in mock lamentation for Queen Victoria's wedding.

Victoria and Albert

On the evening of 10th February 1840, after their wedding in the Chapel Royal, St James's Palace, **Queen Victoria and Prince Albert** drove through cheering crowds to Windsor Castle for a brief honeymoon. So began the close association with Windsor which was to last throughout their lives, an association illustrated by the streets and buildings in the town named after them and their children. From 1850 the Prince was High Steward of the Borough, and the Prince Consort Model Cottages built in the 1850s under his direction, show his concern for the provision of better housing for the poor, whilst the Albert Institute commemorated his interest in providing leisure and educational opportunities.

After the Prince's tragically early death at Windsor in 1861, possibly from typhoid, the Queen forsook Buckingham Palace for Windsor Castle. She became a familiar figure in the town through her daily drives, and maintained her husband's interest in its affairs, pressing for better housing and sanitation. Her jubilees in 1887 and 1897 were enthusiastically celebrated, with triumphal arches erected in the streets, and it was to Windsor that she was brought after her death at Osborne in January 1901 to be buried at Frogmore beside her beloved husband.

Jane Langton

1841   The foundation stone of the British School in New Road (now Victoria Street) was laid by Mr Chariott. The school was to educate 400 children.
Charles Dickens stayed at the White Hart Hotel to recuperate from illness.
Windsor and Eton Choral Society was officially founded (see 1836).
Pte Bernard Crow aged 20 was flogged, for stealing a pair of army boots, until he collapsed and was sent to the military hospital to recover.
Clewer Manor was built.
17th August The annual revel on Bachelors' Acre was described in *The Times*.
Windsor post office moved to a site next to the New Inn in St Albans Street/ Park Street.

1842   A report on an enquiry into the sanitary condition of the labouring population of Great Britain condemned Windsor as the worst, beyond comparison. From the gas works to the end of George Street (now Station Approach) a double line of open deep black and stagnant ditches extended to Clewer Lane. From these ditches an intolerable stench was perpetually rising and produced fever of a severe character.
4th April Prince Albert laid the foundation stone of Holy Trinity Church. The architect was Edward Blore.

1843   Queen Victoria decided to open a school in the Great Park for the children of her employees.

The Crown purchased the Keppel Estate, thus joining Home and Great Parks ensuring unsatisfactory developments did not intrude on the castle.

Dedworth, which had been a detached portion of the parish of Windsor, became part of the parish of Clewer and at the same time the parish of Holy Trinity was created.

1844   *October* Robert Tighe (who was manager of a bank and brewery in Windsor) opened a campaign in the White Hart Inn to form a company to construct an atmospheric railway. Eton College objected and the Commons Committee decided against its construction.

Garrison Church Holy Trinity Church was consecrated by the Bishop of Oxford the Rt Revd the Hon. Richard Bagot. Part of its function was as a garrison church for the soldiers at the two nearby barracks. Sunday church parades became regular attractions for Windsorians, followed by band concerts on the barrack lawn.

Louis Philippe, King of the French, worshipped at the Roman Catholic Chapel in Clewer Green whilst staying at Windsor Castle on a visit to Queen Victoria.

A ragged school was opened in Goswell Lane for poor children who were too poor and unkempt to attend public schools.

Brothers and Clergymen

The **Revd Stephen Hawtrey** MA was the first mathematics master at Eton College and the first incumbent of Holy Trinity Church, Windsor (1844-1866). In 1846 he was joined by his brother, **Henry** as his curate. Together they did what they could for their poor parishioners who lived in slums in Bier Lane when cholera broke out again in 1849. In 1852 Stephen handed over the care of the parish to Henry. Ministry to the soldiers during and after the Crimean War became more important and Henry was responsible for raising the Gallery Memorial recording the names of those who died. The text from the New Testament was chosen by Queen Victoria herself and the Bishop of Oxford inaugurated the Memorial on Advent Sunday 28th November 1863. Meanwhile Stephen oversaw the building of St Anne's School in Alma Road, in 1855, and was founder of St Mark's Day School for Boys in Alma Road. This was so named after being opened on St Mark's Day, 25th April 1862. It became a boarding school in 1870 and later became Imperial Services College Junior School. The boys worshipped at Holy Trinity until their own chapel, now demolished, was built on the site now occupied by Goslar Way. Henry's status was elevated to Rector in 1866 but by 1873 he found the work of a large parish too much for him and exchanged parishes with Revd Arthur Robins, Vicar of Nursling in Hampshire.

Jonathan Cruickshank

1845   *May* A post office was set up at Clewer Green School.

1846   Stephen Hawtrey opened St Mark's School in three rooms in Clewer Lane
        (now Oxford Road). It was modelled on tradesmen's schools.
        The mayor, James Bedborough, called a meeting at the Guildhall to discuss the
        merits of the Great Western and South Western Railway's proposals for
        Windsor. The meeting broke up in disorder.
        Princess Helena, the fifth child of Queen Victoria, was born. She later
        became Princess Christian and was known as The Windsor Princess.

1847   Royal Assent given to the Windsor, and South Western Railway Bill. The bells
        of the parish church were rung in celebration.
        A military prison was built at the back of the cavalry barracks.
        The borough jail was in Sheet Street (Governor John Sims) and the police
        station in Church Street (Superintendent William Gillman).
        By this time Caleys was at 19 High Street, where it is today.

Charismatic Cleric

Thomas Thellusson Carter (1808-1901) was born at Eton, younger son of Revd Thomas Carter, vice-Provost of Eton and his wife Mary, daughter of Henry Proctor of Clewer. He was educated at Eton and Christchurch Oxford, and was a friend and contemporary of Gladstone. After his ordination he became his father's curate at Burnham, Bucks. He married Mary Gould and they had three children. After a short period as Rector of Piddlehinton in Dorset he became Rector of Clewer in 1844. The parish was large with poverty near the town centre and wealth outside the town. With two barracks nearby and navvies building the new railways there was the problem of prostitution.

In 1849 Mariquita Tennant, a widow living near Carter's church, took in an abused young woman and thus began the Clewer House of Mercy. In 1851 Mrs Tennant gave up the work because of poor health, but Carter persuaded another widow, Harriet Monsell, to take over. Together they founded the Community of St John the Baptist with Harriet Monsell as Mother Superior and Carter as Warden, the main work being moral rescue.

Carter remained Rector of Clewer until 1880 when he resigned because of objections to his high church ritual, culminating in a famous court case in which he was supported by his bishop. He remained Sisters' Warden until his death on 28th October 1901, and is buried in Clewer Churchyard. Well respected in wider church circles, Carter pioneered retreats, wrote numerous devotional and theological books and was a conciliator in a time of religious controversy.

Valerie Bonham

1848   Death of Joseph Chariott, at the age of 91. He was a member of the William
Street Congregational Chapel. In his will he left money for the building of
almshouses, now known as Chariotts Charity.
The Windsor Castle and Town Approaches Act was passed, leading to new
roads and bridges and an improved setting for the castle.
The passing of the Public Health Act brought hopes for the improvement to
the health of Windsor inhabitants.
At the magistrates' court held in the Guildhall a lad called David Howick was
sentenced to be privately whipped for robbing the till of Mr Eden, a baker.

1849   Brunel's wrought-iron bowstring girder bridge was built over the Thames for
the railway. Windsor Great Western Station was built by Brunel.
23rd November The Royal train - from Windsor to Basingstoke - was
driven by Sir Daniel Gooch.

Engineering Genius

Daniel Gooch (1816-1889) spent his childhood in the village of Bedlington in Northumberland
near Stephenson's Birkinshaw Ironworks where he served an engineering apprenticeship. When
he was only 21 he was appointed Locomotive Superintendent of the Great Western Railway by
Isambard Kingdom Brunel, and it was Gooch's brilliance which led to safer and speedier trains. In
1864 he resigned as Locomotive Superintendent to inaugurate telegraphic communication between
England and America and he despatched the first cable message across the Atlantic in 1866.
Queen Victoria created him a baronet in the same year. Sir Daniel was chairman of the GWR from
1865 and supported the building of the Great Eastern steamship and construction of the Severn
Tunnel. He became MP for Cricklade and Deputy Lieutenant for Wiltshire. As a Berkshire JP he
served on the bench at the Windsor Guildhall Quarter Sessions.

   In 1859 he bought Clewer Park and rebuilt the cottages in Mill Lane for his workers and
a plaque was erected on one of these by Windsor Local History Publications Group in memory of
Gooch as his house was demolished in 1956. He also rebuilt the front of the Swan Public House.
He loved Clewer so much that he chose the site of his tomb in Clewer churchyard in the mid-
1860s, 25 years before his death. This has become a site of pilgrimage for many railway enthusiasts.

Sheila Rooney

Cholera reached Windsor after sweeping through Europe. There were about
1000 cases in the town and 25 deaths. Dr Geoffrey Pearl who was the visiting
surgeon at the infirmary wrote to the *Windsor Express* stressing the wisdom
of isolating patients and districts during epidemics.

1849
cont.
December 29th Mariquita Tennant, a widow living at The Limes near Clewer Church, took in an abused young woman and thus began the Clewer House of Mercy.
She offered shelter to young women and girls trying to escape from the appalling conditions in the slum areas of the town.

Mariquita Tennant

The Water was Bad! Following the receipt of a petition signed by 228 ratepayers stating that the sewerage and drainage was deficient, an investigation was carried out by Edward Cresy. His report to the General Board of Health showed that Windsor was one of the most insanitary towns in the country and proposed improvements.

1849
"A young girl was executed at Windsor on Monday. This wretched criminal underwent the extreme penalty of the law on Monday morning, the scene throughout was a most painful one. Half an hour previous to the event the governor of the gaol announced to her the painful duty he had to perform and hoped she would accompany him to the scaffold quietly, she stamped her feet and said she would not go. He was compelled to procure the assistance of six or seven men. She struggled violently and shrieked in a dreadful manner and when the executioner put the rope around her neck she screamed 'Lord have mercy upon me.' The bolt was withdrawn and the poor young woman was launched into eternity." *Windsor Express 22nd April 1849.*

1850
New Drains Ready A new drainage system for the town was completed. Prince Albert formed the Royal Society for the Improvement of the Conditions of the Labouring Classes leading to the improvement of housing and the building of Prince Consort Cottages.
There was a public telegraph at 48 High Street until 1854.

1851   The Clewer House of Mercy moved to Nightingale Place, Hatch Lane.
Windsor formed its own board of health.
Construction began on a system of underground sewers, but this system had a major defect in that there was no ventilation for the drains.
Guildhall restoration began.
Station Opened The South Western Railway's Riverside Station was opened after the railway was extended from Black Potts. The station was designed by Sir William Tite and had large doors to enable soldiers to march in and out.

1852   Houses in Bier Lane (now River Street) were flooded for 17 days.
The last public well and pump was built in Datchet Road.
Probably the last duel in England was fought between two Frenchmen on Priest Hill, Old Windsor. One man was killed and the other was sentenced for manslaughter.

30th November Harriet Monsell was installed as the first Superior of the Community of St John the Baptist, Clewer, formed to supervise the work of the House of Mercy.

Harriet Monsell as a young woman

1853   *26th March* **Fire at Windsor Castle** in the north-east corner damaged the state dining room and the Prince of Wales Tower. Two fire engines arrived from London by rail to supplement the six volunteer brigades.
July Edward Lear stayed at the Prince Albert Public House in Clewer Green to paint the view from St Leonard's Hill for the Earl of Derby. He grumbled about the dusty roads and changeable weather.
Major restoration of St Andrew's Church Clewer was begun by the architect Henry Woodyer. The church was in such a bad state that the first proposal was to erect a new building. The restoration was to take five years.

1853
cont.

Graveyards ordered to be closed because they were full and had become a health hazard.

The ragged school needed to expand and new premises in Clarence Lane (later Oxford Road) were given by Alderman Bedborough.

13 High Street, Windsor, which was set up as a photography studio in 1852. The large windows on the first floor were needed to let in daylight before electricity. There are very few examples of such studios still in existence.

1854   St Leonard's was bought by Mr Brinkman.

The first set of regulations 'The Statutes of the House of Mercy, Clewer' for the governing of the community of St John the Baptist was issued.

1855   The Prince Consort Model Cottages, based on designs by Henry Roberts at the 1851 Great Exhibition, were built by the Royal Windsor Society to provide good quality living accommodation for working men and their families.

The Emperor Napoleon III visited Windsor with Empress Eugenie. The South Western Railway station was illuminated with gas jets so that the words **WELCOME NAPOLEON** flared out and was greatly admired.

29th November The Bishop of Oxford, the Rt Revd Samuel Wilberforce, blessed and opened the first stage of the new buildings on the Nightingale Place estate in Hatch Lane to accommodate the House of Mercy and the Community of St John the Baptist, the architect being Henry Woodyer.

1856   End of the Crimean War. Many of the fatalities are recorded in Holy Trinity Church where the lists show that more soldiers died from disease than wounds. A number of faded and fragile banners hang in the church.

1857   Both Windsor barracks were condemned as unhealthy, overcrowded and having appalling sanitary arrangements.
Windsor Infirmary was established adjoining Bachelors' Acre, opposite the barracks.

1858   *26th March* The new town cemetery at Spital was consecrated by the Bishop of Oxford Rt Revd Samuel Wilberforce. It was open to all denominations.
18th May St John's Home for Orphans was opened by Bishop Wilberforce.
Typhoid epidemic. The Queen's Physician, Sir James Clark reported that good water was available in the town but three fifths of the population were drawing their water from surface wells which were polluted by waste.

1st July **House of Mercy Dedicated** The new buildings at the House of Mercy were dedicated by Bishop Wilberforce. There were 800 people present and a special train was run from Paddington.

The work of restoring St Andrew's Church Clewer was finished.
Dr William Brown Holderness was appointed surgeon to the dispensary and infirmary.
The Local Government Act gave wider powers to the borough to regulate the building of houses.
The Annals of Windsor by Robert Richard Tighe and James Edward Davies was published, and the two volumes are still the mainstay of historical research of Windsor.

1859   The National School and (Royal) Free School amalgamated and work began on a new school building on Bachelors' Acre.

1860   Separate accommodation for married families was first provided in the Windsor barracks. Families no longer had to share quarters with the men in the barrack rooms.
Darvilles opened their first store in Peascod Street.
A public meeting raised £800 for the suffering caused by the Indian Mutiny.

1861   Beaumont Lodge Old Windsor was bought by the Jesuits and became a Roman Catholic School.
The Royal Free School re-opened on Bachelors' Acre (now flats).

1861 **Death of Prince Albert** The town was stunned by the news of the Prince
cont. Albert's death from typhoid. Many people heard the news as they emerged
from church on Sunday morning.

23rd December The Prince was buried in the Royal Vault under St George's
Chapel, but a week later Queen Victoria started preparations for the Royal
Mausoleum at Frogmore to receive the Prince's coffin.

1862 Canon Ellison announced that the parish church was too small. A new church
(All Saints, Frances Road) was approved by Queen Victoria. Arthur
Blomfield was commissioned to design the building. His student, Thomas
Hardy visited the site to make the necessary drawings, which can still be seen
in the church.

The foundation stone of the first All Saints Church, Dedworth was laid. It
was built as a memorial to Mary Sophie Tudor by her husband and children.
The church, designed by G F Bodley, contained stained glass windows by
William Morris, Edward Burne-Jones, Dante Gabriel Rossetti and Ford
Madox-Brown, members of the pre-Raphaelite movement.
St Mark's School had moved to Alma Road and there were 57 boys. Revd
Henry Moseley, Her Majesty's Inspector, visited the school and praised it.

1863 *10th March* For the marriage of the Prince of Wales and Alexandra of
Denmark, local Sunday School children gathered outside the castle to sing
'God Bless the Prince of Wales'.
July All Saints Church Dedworth was consecrated by the Bishop of Oxford.
A council report condemned the water in four of the town's wells as unfit for
human consumption.
21st November The foundation stone of All Saints Church, Frances Road
was laid by the Princess Royal, Crown Princess of Prussia. Thomas Hardy
attended the ceremony and supervised the building.

1864 *21st November* All Saints Church Frances Road was consecrated by
Bishop Wilberforce.
The old Royal Free School building became a Masonic hall.
A small hoard of bronze axes was found in Windsor Great Park.
The first Magdalen was consecrated at Clewer House of Mercy. These were
girls who has been rescued by the Sisters and wanted to remain at the
convent. A separate sisterhood was created for them.

1865 The Infantry barracks were extended over Spring Gardens and Barrack Lane
(work continued until 1867).

1865 The Cavalry barracks were extended and partially re-built after a visit by
cont. Queen Victoria who was appalled by the conditions her soldiers had to
endure. The cost was £30,000.
Margaret Oliphant, Scottish novelist, moved into 6 Clarence Crescent.

Thomas Hardy (1840-1928) and All Saints Church Windsor

All Saints Church stands at the junction of Alexandra Road and Frances Road, a mile from the Castle. In 1862 Canon Ellison, Vicar of Windsor, announced that the seating in the parish church in the High Street was proving inadequate. Many poorer parishioners could not afford the pew rents. The plan for a new church was approved by Queen Victoria who contributed £300, and signified her pleasure that her daughter, the Princess Royal, would lay the foundation stone. Mr (later Sir) Arthur Blomfield, the eminent architect, was commissioned for the work. He sent his young apprentice **Thomas Hardy**, who later achieved fame as a novelist, to visit the site to make the necessary plans and drawings (these were discovered at the back of the organ in the parish church in the mid 1970s and can be seen at All Saints today). By 21st November 1863, when the foundation stone was laid, subscriptions had risen to £3,400. The ceremony was a happy occasion as the Princess celebrated her 23rd birthday. Exactly one year later, on 21st November 1864, a grander event took place: the consecration of the church. Accompanying her Royal Highness from the Castle was a numerous and brilliant royal party, who joined a host of local people. Bishop Wilberforce of Oxford preached a sermon entitled 'The need was great'. The final cost of the church was £4000, with seating for 600. Mother and daughter churches have always worked as one parish.

Ellen Dollery

1866 *5th July* The streets of Windsor were decorated for the wedding of Princess
Helena to Prince Christian of Schleswig-Holstein-Sonderbourg-Augustenburg.
30th November. St Andrew's Convalescent Hospital, Hatch Lane, run by the
Community of St John the Baptist, was opened by Bishop Wilberforce.
The bronze axes found in Windsor Great Park two years earlier, and other
local items, were given by Queen Victoria to form the nucleus of a Windsor
museum.
Racing began on Rays Island, the site of the present Windsor Racecourse,
promoted by John Frail.

1867 *4th February* At the first meeting of Windsor Volunteer Fire Brigade William
Mason was elected as captain.
31st December Royal Albert Institute Trust was founded.
The headmaster of Eton tried to stop a performance at the Theatre Royal
because Eton boys were in the audience.

1868   *13th October*   The Church of St Edward, King and Confessor, in Alma Road was dedicated by the Archbishop of Westminster, Henry Manning. It was designed by Charles Alban Buckler and replaced the Chapel in Hermitage Lane, Clewer Green. This Chapel, owned and built by the Riley family, was sold to provide money for the new building

29th October   St Stephen's Mission House was opened and blessed by Revd TT Carter. The building was used for St Stephen's Ragged School.

Windsor and Eton Waterworks Act.

Windsor loses one MP   Under the Parliamentary Reform Act the number of MPs representing Windsor was reduced from two to one.

Windsor, along with other garrison towns, came under the Contagious Diseases Acts. This meant that all prostitutes within ten miles of the town could be forcibly examined and put into locked wards if found diseased. Soldiers on the other hand, were now exempt from regular medical inspections. The CD Acts were abolished because of public pressure in 1879.

The Duke's Head, at the corner of Peascod Street and Clewer Lane, was pulled down. It had been used for theatrical performances at some time.

1869   **Floods!**

28th October   The lease was signed for a piece of land at Dedworth to be used by the Dedworth branch of the Fifield Baptist Mission. The first chapel, known as 'the Old Tin Chapel', was erected on this site.

Albert Remembered

The Royal Albert Institute Trust was founded in 1867 to provide "amongst other necessary rooms a Commodious Lecture Hall capable of holding at least 500 persons". Life membership of ten guineas provided the finance and Queen Victoria took great interest in its progress. The objects preserved today were "to promote the study of literature, science and the fine arts and the delivery of lectures on subjects of general interest". Up to 1939 the Institute flourished, but the postwar television culture starved it of support. After the County Education Committee moved out the Trustees sold the property in 1968. Alderman Tozer, former Mayor, became Chairman and John Handcock became Clerk to the Trustees and the Charity Commissioners approved a reconstructed scheme.

    At March 2000 the Trust capital stood at over £100,000 and grants to local organisations are running at approximately £7,500 per annum. Recently the Trust has assisted in the renovation of the George V and the Prince Christian memorials, the Observatory constructed by the Herschel Astronomical Society in Eton and the Parish Church clock besides contributing to the Choral Society, the Operatic Society, Eton Wick Village History Group for the Folly Bridge Pound, the Clewer Museum and many others. The Trust's major millennium project consisted of £5,000 towards the Parish Church revitalisation. It is felt that in these ways the Prince Consort will continue to be remembered as it is felt he would have wished.

John Handcock

Windsor's Scottish Novelist

Margaret Oliphant (1828-1897) novelist, critic and biographer, lived in Clarence Crescent for thirty years. As a widow with two sons she came to the town in 1865, choosing it for ' the beauty of the river and the castle and the air of cheerful life about'. The family moved into 6 Clarence Crescent, a house which Mrs Oliphant loved for its sunny aspect and the communal garden where her boys could play. Behind the back wall were some of Windsor's worst slums, but no reference can be found in her *Autobiography* or letters to them. Mrs Oliphant had to work extremely hard at her writing to pay Eton fees and maintain a rather grand life-style, especially after her brother and his family became dependent on her as well. She bought 8-9 Clarence Crescent to accommodate them all (a plaque was placed there to mark her centenary). Her prolific writings were much liked by Queen Victoria (the best are probably her Carlingford novels, including *Miss Marjoribanks,* and her ghost stories). The Queen invited her to tea in the castle on several occasions, describing her as 'simple, quiet and intelligent' and awarding her a pension of £100 a year. Unfortunately Mrs Oliphant's last years were made unhappy by the indolence of her sons. Both predeceased her, after which she could no longer bear to live in the once happy house and moved away.

Hester Davenport

1870   A chancel was added to Windsor Parish Church.

9th November Work began on Clewer St Stephen's Church, Vansittart Road. An Education Act was passed which allowed local authorities to raise money from the rates to provide elementary schools. However, no school board was set up in Windsor because it was so well provided with schools by the church.

Princess Christian set up a nursery in Grove Road with Miss Oxley. It was for the children of working mothers.
Princess Christian was appointed Chairman of the Ladies Committee for Aid to Sick and Wounded Soldiers, which predated the British Red Cross.
Prince Christian of Schleswig-Holstein was made High Steward of Windsor.

1871   *25th July* The completed part of Clewer St Stephen's Church opened.
Sewage was delivered to the sewage farm at Ham Island in Old Windsor.

The British Infants School was opened

1872   The poor sanitary conditions at the Windsor Cavalry barracks were discussed in parliament.
Sir Francis Tress Barry bought St. Leonard's Hill and re-built it.
Margaret Oliphant moved from 6 Clarence Crescent to 8-9.
St Anne's Infant School was opened.

Temperance Reformer

 **Frederic Rainer** (1836-1911) was born in Queen Street, now Market Street. His father was a stonemason and the family lived above Rainer's Eating House which was run by his mother. He attended the National School in Garfield Place until he was ten when he was given a place in the Free School in Church Street. In the area in which he grew up he witnessed the terrible drunkeness and violence which led to so much misery and unhappiness amongst the poor. When the Revd Henry Ellison formed the Church of England Temperance Society in 1868 Frederic became one of its members. He was also associated with the National Police Court Mission which eventually became the modern Probation Service. A plaque which was placed on the outside wall of the Guildhall commemorates his work in Windsor.

Sheila Rooney

1873   The Shah of Persia visited Windsor and was so impressed with the gas lighting that he asked to see the gas works.
St Stephen's Schools opened for infants, boys and girls. They were founded by the nuns of the Convent of St John the Baptist, Clewer.
Gates in memory of Charles Knight were erected on Bachelors' Acre.

1874   *1st September* Spital Infants School opened in St Leonard's Road.
24th September Ceremonial opening of the completed St Stephen's Church.
22nd December Clewer St Stephen's Church was consecrated by the Rt Revd John Mackarness, Bishop of Oxford.
St Agnes' Church, Spital was built. Canon Carter, Rector of Clewer, paid for the building. The architect is thought to have been Stephen Wyborn.

The Windsor Princess

Princess Helena (1846-1923), the fifth of Queen Victoria's children and the third daughter. She was only fifteen when her father died and she became an indispensable secretary to her bereaved mother. Her father's influence on her was to show itself when she spent a great deal of her adult life caring for the people of Windsor. In 1866 she married Prince Christian of Schleswig-Holstein and they lived for most of their life in Cumberland Lodge in Windsor Great Park. **Princess Christian**, as she was now known, became concerned first of all with the welfare of poor children and helped Miss Oxley with her nursery for the children of destitute mothers. Her greatest work was in the field of nursing where she opened a home for the training of nurses at 1 and 2 Clarence Villas and in 1900 she bought numbers 3 and 4 Clarence Villas in memory of her son Prince Christian Victor who had died in the Boer War. This became the Princess Christian Nursing Home.

Kathleen Whelan

1874   Alexander II, Czar of all the Russias, arrived at the South Western Railway
        station at 9.30 in the evening for a state visit. The station was 'brilliantly
        illuminated' with artificial light. He was escorted to the castle by the
        Coldstream Guards and the 1st Life Guards.

1875   The police station was in Sheet Street. The superintendent was George Hays
        and there were 2 sergeants and 13 constables. Prisoners committed for trial
        were sent to Reading.
        Mother Harriet retired as Superior of the Community of St John the Baptist.

1876   *8th May* The foundation stone of the Weslyan Methodist Chapel, Alma Road
        was laid. The architect was Joseph Morris of Messrs Morris and Stallwood of
        Reading.

A Generous Benefactor

Sir Francis Tress Barry (1825-1907) made a fortune in Portuguese copper mining. He was created
Baron Barry of Portugal and in 1872 was Consul General in England for the Republic of Ecuador.
He bought St Leonard's Hill from the Harcourt estate and lavishly embellished it in the French
style to make it look like a French Chateau. Tress Barry was a generous benefactor to many good
causes in the Borough of New Windsor, particularly the infirmary, where from 1876 he was an
annual subscriber. The accident ward, later known as the Barry Ward, was set up when he donated
£1,000 for its establishment. Queen Victoria created him a baronet and awarded him the Jubilee
Medal and bar. Between 1890 and 1906 he served as MP for Windsor. He died in 1907 and is
buried in Clewer parish churchyard. Barry Avenue is named after him.

Sheila Rooney

The Royal Windsor Tapestry Manufactory opened in Old Windsor, under the
patronage of Prince Leopold. Low warp looms were used by workers who
came from Aubusson in France. Most of the tapestries were commissioned
by the Royal Family but it was never a commercial success.

A borough byelaw made school attendance compulsory for all Windsor
children between the ages of 5 and 10, and, for those up to 13 unless they
could pass the fifth standard examination.
St Saviour's Church, River Street, was built as a district church of Holy
Trinity. The church, which was built by public subscription, was designed by
Stephen Wyborn.
St Stephen's High School opened.

Floods of 1873 and 1875

DELIVERING COAL

TEMPORARY BRIDGES.

POSTAL DELIVERY.

Queen Victoria pictured in 1875. When Prince Albert died she appeared entirely in black,
but by this year she had lighened her widow's weeds with white cap and frills.

1877 *21st February* The Wesleyan Methodist Chapel, Alma Road, opened.
Royal Free Infants School opened..

1880 *10th January* **Royal Albert Institute Opened** The Royal Albert Institute
in Sheet Street was opened by the Prince of Wales, providing the town with a
centre for cultural activities.

Picture-makers in Wool

 Set back from the Straight Road which runs through Old Windsor is an attractive black and white timbered building, once the premises of the **Royal Windsor Tapestry Manufactory**. Encouraged by Queen Victoria's youngest son Prince Leopold, two Frenchmen, Henri CJ Henry and Marcel Brignolas, had in 1876 brought over workers from the famous Aubusson works in France and set up their looms, initially in Manor Lodge on the other side of the road. The workers' wives became tapestry repairers, and a school was set up at the Lord Nelson public house for the French children. The pub also housed the vats for dyeing the wools, and the Manufactory boasted that it could produce 5,000 different shades of colour.

At first the enterprise was very successful, winning a gold medal at the Paris Exhibition of 1878 with a lively series of tapestries showing scenes from Shakespeare's *The Merry Wives of Windsor*. The RWTM also introduced portraiture to tapestries with one of Queen Victoria, while another showed Henry Irving and Ellen Terry in a scene from *Romeo and Juliet*. With success came the building of the Tapestry Hall which had a central hall to display the tapestries and 12 attached cottages for the workers. English apprentices were taken on, and at Manor Lodge Cottage Henri Henry developed another business, the Royal Windsor Stained Glass Manufactory. This produced some fine windows, including two in the Guildhall which portray Prince Leopold and Princess Beatrice.

Unfortunately Prince Leopold, the RWTM's President, died in 1884, and without his support the Manufactory went into decline, closing its doors on Christmas Eve 1890. The building today is known as The Tapestries and provides accommodation for the elderly.

Hester Davenport

Herbert George (HG) Wells was employed for 2 months as an apprentice draper's assistant at Messrs Rodgers and Denyer's store in the High Street. He hated the job and was dismissed because his carelessness led to thefts from his till.

Queensmead, now the home of Brigidine Convent, was built for Henri Henry manager of the Royal Windsor Tapestry Manufactory with windows made at the stained glass factory. These windows can still be seen in the building.

Francis Tress Barry was elected as MP for Windsor.

1881   *25th May* Old Windsor Working Men's Club premises were opened by Lady Julia Follett. The club was founded by Colonel Follett and Dr AP Shaw.
9th July A Grand Volunteer Review was held in Windsor Great Park. Queen Victoria reviewed 52,000 citizen soldiers.
Wellesley Home opened for penitents waiting to get places in penitentiaries.

20th October A new, larger chapel, designed by Henry Woodyer was dedicated by the Rt Revd John Mackarness, Bishop of Oxford for the Community of St John the Baptist. The original chapel, dedicated in 1855, had become too small.

The chapel of the Forerunner as it was in 1882, looking east.

1883   *17th March* Lady Florence Dixie, travel writer and the first woman war correspondent, believed she was the victim of an Irish Republican assassination attempt at her home at the Fishery, Maidenhead Road. The event became headline news in the national press.

Slough Observer founded by Charles Luff. There is now a Windsor edition of this newspaper. TE Luff bought 47 St Leonard's Road where the family traded as printers and stationers for over a hundred years.
St Augustine's Home Clewer founded by the Community of St John the Baptist as an orphanage for boys.

1884   *January* 36 unemployed workmen were given a free supper at the Star Inn in Peascod Street. They had recently been employed building St Edward's house next to St Edward's Church.
Windsor Corporation Water Act was passed. This enabled the corporation to take control of the water supply and in 1888 they acquired the water works. The Board of Health began to seal up contaminated wells.

1885   *The Lancet* sent a special commissioner to investigate the condition of the poorer parts of Windsor and he wrote a damning report.
Wilde Deplores Corsets Oscar Wilde gave a lecture on dress at the Royal Albert Institute. He recommended that ancient Greek costume should be adopted. He particularly deplored the use of corsets.
Dysons took over the jewellers shop at 9 Thames Street.

1886   The Cemetery Chapel at Old Windsor was built.
Clewer New Town Sub-Post Office opened.

Princess Christian recognised the need for nurses to be trained and employed Miss Wade, who had already received training. The Princess also set up a fund called the Free Dinner and Relief Fund and spent £150 on meals, coal and blankets for the poor.

1887   *19th February* A new post office was opened in the High Street opposite the old one. At that time this office handled all the royal post.
17th June **Queen Victoria's Golden Jubilee.**
20th June The town was decorated and illuminated for the Jubilee. In the afternoon a troop of Royal Horse Guards perfomed a musical ride in the Home Park and in the evening a huge bonfire was lit and kept fed with tar barrels. An ox was roasted, not very successfully, for distribution amongst the poor.
21st June A Venetian Fete was held with hundreds of boats adorned with Chinese lanterns and coloured lamps lit up at dusk which sailed in procession up and down the river. In the evening there was a magnificent display of fireworks and the castle was adorned with electric lights and coloured fire on the Round Tower.
22nd June The town was thronged with people to watch Queen Victoria drive through the town to unveil the statue of herself which had been erected at the bottom of Castle Hill. The statue, which was by J E Boehm, had been paid for by subscriptions from the residents of Windsor.
June 23rd Six thousand children aged 6 - 14 from schools in Windsor and nearby were given dinner and tea in the private part of the Home Park. The Queen and several members of her family drove past them as they were drawn up under the trees. There was a display of fire engines with the fireman and their horses later taking part in a torchlight procession to the Castle Quadrangle.

1888   **Waterworks Acquired by the Corporation**. £131,000 was paid to the trustees of the Cutler family who had run the waterworks for 141 years. Christopher Sainty was the new water engineer.

Sir Francis Tress Barry

1888 As Lord of the Manor of several areas in Windsor, Queen Victoria owned
cont. much of the land. She sold this land to individual and corporate buyers. One of
these manors was Dedworth Maunsell and she sold the rent of the Wolf
public house at Dedworth to Margaretta, widow of Henry Vansittart
Penefather. The lady was in Natal, South Africa, at the time so Bucklands,
the estate agents, managed the property for her.
Butler & Son, furniture emporium, opened in St Leonard's Road.

1889 The Royal Agricultural Society of England held their 50th Annual Exhibition in
Windsor Great Park.

1890 Because of the terrible winter a charity was set up to distribute soup and
bread to the poor three times a week. Princess Christian helped in the kitchen
at the Guildhall.
A post office was set up in the castle to handle royal post, which had
previously been handled in the town office.
A great frost began at the end of the year.

1891 The great frost continued. The Thames was frozen and skaters made use of
the ice.
May Electric lighting, 'even in the stables' was advertised by the White Hart
Hotel. This was supplied via a cable across the roofs, as the council would not
give permission to dig up the pavement in High Street and Peascod Street.

1892 *December* Windsor Electrical Supply Company arranged for a gang of men
to arrive very early in the morning and dig up High Street, Peascod Street and
Thames Street to lay cables. They were prosecuted and fined £9.16s.

Catholic Canon

Canon John Longinetto was most influential in the development of St Edward's Roman Catholic Church in Alma Road. Not only did he have a profound effect on the growth of the Catholic presence in Windsor but he also played a vigorous part in the life of the town as a whole. Canon Longinetto (then Father) came to Windsor as parish priest in 1889 at the age of 32 and during the next 47 years he extended the church, built a permanent school in the church grounds and was a valued member of the Windsor Education Committee. When he arrived in the parish he found a beautiful church, which had been built largely through the generosity of Count Ramon de Morella, but there was only a temporary school housed in a lean-to building where the sanctuary now stands. There was obviously a great need for a permanent school and Canon Longinetto made this one of his main ambitions together with the enlargement and beautification of the church. A previous incumbent, Canon Applegath, had built the three main bays of the church and Longinetto's first task was to add to the sanctuaries and the vestries together with the shrines, the reredos and many of the stained glass windows. He then turned his attention to the building of the school and it was duly opened in 1898 with him as the first manager and chairman. Canon Longinetto was a member of Windsor Education Committee from its inception and Chairman from 1909. He was an acknowledged expert in the field of Italian art and literature and frequently gave lectures to the Royal Albert Institute of which he was at some time Vice President. He left Windsor in 1936 when he retired to Brighton and is buried in Brighton cemetery.

Barbara Mitch

1893 The corporation began to deal with the squalid piles of rubbish which spoiled the riverside.

March **Smallpox at Clewer** An epidemic of smallpox broke out in Clewer and the rector, Roland Errington, arranged for marquees to be erected in a field behind the rectory to isolate the patients. Nurse Shaddock worked in the marquees for the whole seven months of the crisis.

1894 The Local Government Act led to the formation of civil parishes and parish councils. In the area covered by this book there were two, Clewer and Old Windsor.

4th December At Old Windsor the overseer of the poor, Mr Blake, convened a meeting to elect a parish council, and 95 people attended. Nine councillors were elected by a show of hands but several dissatisfied people demanded a secret poll. There was another election but not all the previously elected councillors were re-elected.

Disastrous flood.

St Edward's Roman Catholic School was opened on land to the rear of the church in Dorset Road.

Barclays Bank opened on the present site in High Street on the corner of Peascod Street.

1894 HRH Princess Christian founded a hospital at 12 Clarence Road.
cont.   Records of Windsor's first telephone exchange date from 1894.
       The National Telephone Company was in Datchet Road at that time.
       The first edition of Windsor's Telephone Directory had five numbers:
           1   Rodgers & Denyers Silk Mercers, High Street Windsor
           2   Caley & Son High St Windsor
           3   Willis & Son Cycle Manufacturers 124 High Street Eton
           4   Brook & Son Store Peascod Street Windsor
           5   Call Room - Toomer & Son High Street Windsor

1895   Probationers first accepted for training as nurses.
       First meeting of Old Windsor Parish Council.
       The First Car on an English Road The Hon. Evelyn Ellis of Datchet
       drove from Micheldever in Hampshire to Datchet passing through Windsor on
       the route. It was the first time any car had been driven on an English Road.

1896   *7th July* Trooper Thomas Charles Wooldridge of the Royal Horse Guards,
       who murdered his wife in Arthur Road, Windsor, was hanged in Reading gaol.
       His execution inspired Oscar Wilde to write *The Ballad of Reading Gaol.*

Architect and Artist

In 1867 **Alfred Young Nutt** (1847- 1924) moved to Windsor from Leicester to work as an architect at Windsor Castle. A water-colour artist, he was particularly attracted to painting views of Windsor from the river, at different times of the year. He was in great demand in the town to create illuminated addresses and these include paintings of many parts of the town. AY Nutt had a flair for designing ceremonial arches, best seen when he created a ceremonial route in Windsor for Queen Victoria's Diamond Jubilee.

Artist and Photographer

George Moore Henton (1861-1924) lived in Leicester and stayed in Windsor with the Nutt family. In the 1890s he painted a series of street scenes for publication in two books, but his great contribution to recording life in Windsor comes from a collection of photographs of Windsor and Eton. Some of these photographs were preparation work for his paintings. All social groups and classes are represented including haymakers and shoe-blacks. His studies of children are excellent. The photographs are all dated and many of them are marked with the time and weather conditions. Originals and copies of work by both artists can be seen at the Royal Borough Museum Collection.

Norman Oxley

Maid and Child watching the Coldstream Guards

May 1894 - George Henton

Organ Grinder and Cutler in Bier Lane May 1894 - George Henton

1897   *23rd June* Queen Victoria's Diamond Jubilee was celebrated in London
24th June The Queen arrived at Slough by train and travelled by coach to
Windsor. There was a tumultuous welcome from huge crowds lining the route
through Eton. Many country people joined the crowds and their horses and
carts parked in adjoining fields caused traffic chaos. Several spectacular
decorative arches spanned the roads. A temporary canopy adorned her statue
and buildings were hung with flags. There were bonfires, fireworks,
illuminations and massed choirs.

*The fire brigades assembled at the Home Park and marched
with lighted torches, as shown in the picture, around the town
and to Eton accompanied by a Brass Band.*

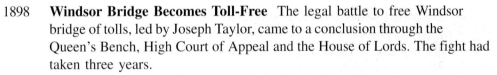

25th June A torchlight procession of Eton
College boys marched to the Upper Ward at
Windsor Castle.
Windsor Division of the St John Ambulance
Brigade formed.
30th June Old Windsor Methodist Church
opened.
Work began on the rebuilding of Windsor
Central station, which took two years.

1898   **Windsor Bridge Becomes Toll-Free** The legal battle to free Windsor
bridge of tolls, led by Joseph Taylor, came to a conclusion through the
Queen's Bench, High Court of Appeal and the House of Lords. The fight had
taken three years.
1st December The tollgates were demolished. The following verse
celebrated the event:

> The task is o'er, the work is done,
> The Gate is lost, the Bridge is won!
> No Tax or Toll shall the Counties part;
> Thus Berks and Bucks unite in heart;
> Windsor and Eton from blight are free,
> Joined by the English gift of Liberty!

The Watch Committee agreed to allow one plain clothes police officer, as and
when necessary.
St Edward's Free Elementary School for mixed juniors and infants was
opened in Dorset Road.
Old Windsor Football Club was formed.

Oxley's Express

Richard Oxley joined the staff of the Windsor Express only a few years after it was started by Charles Knight and in 1835 became sole proprietor. He moved the paper to 4 High Street in 1838 and this remained the head office for nearly 150 years. He ran the paper until 1873 when he handed it over to his son **Frederick William Oxley**. Frederick was succeeded by his son **Stanley Frederick Oxley** in 1902 when he was only 28 years old. Stanley brought modern methods into the newspaper. In 1911 he introduced mechanical typesetting and installed a new press in 1924. He made the firm into a limited company in 1934 and was the first chairman. On his death his wife took over as chairman and held the position for over 20 years.

Pamela Marson

1899   **Windsor to Folkestone in Two and a Half Hours!**
22nd February A train ran from Windsor to Folkestone via Kensington. It left Windsor at 11 am and arrived at Folkestone Harbour at 1.33 pm.
June The Navy League acquired a training vessel which was moored in a backwater below the Great Western Railway bridge. Instructor Mr G Moore started with 12 boys and the number had increased to 25 by October. This was the beginning of the whole Sea Cadet movement. It was the idea of Sir John Soundy, the mayor and funded by Sir Francis Tress Barry.

23 Trinity Place was purchased by Princess Christian Hospital and used as a maternity home for the wives of soldiers who were serving in South Africa. The Infantry barracks was re-named the Victoria Barracks.

1900   Nurses from the Princess Christian Home for Nurses left for the Boer War. The Princess Christian Hospital train (funded by donations from Windsor and Canada) was sent to South Africa to transport the casualties.
On the Relief of Mafeking rockets were fired from the old fire station (then in St Leonard's Road), Sheet Street and the recreation ground.

The Slums are Still With Us! Dr H Timbrell Bulstrode reported on the sanitary condition of the borough and concluded that the situation was dire. A hundred houses in the Goswells were unfit for habitation. The source of the problem was poverty which was due to the fact that Windsor had no industry. Cavalry barracks named Combermere Barracks, in honour of former Gold Stick Viscount Combermere.
PC McLain was appointed Windsor's first detective officer, with extra pay of one shilling a week.

Two Watercolours by AY Nutt - the lower one is
The Bells of Ouseley at Old Windsor

107

1901   *22nd January* Queen Victoria died at Osborne in the Isle of Wight.

23rd January The Prince of Wales was proclaimed King Edward VII.

2nd February The coffin was placed on the Great Western train for Windsor at Paddington Station. The Royal Waiting Room at Windsor's Great Western Station was full of flowers and outside stood the gun carriage on which the coffin would be carried to St George's Chapel, watched by the new King and the Royal Family plus many mourners. The train was half an hour late and the mourners and horses were cold and edgy. As the signal was given for the commencement of the procession one of the horses reared up and caused confusion during which the traces of the gun carriage were broken. Prince Louis Battenberg suggested the Naval Guard of Honour should pull the gun carriage and so the procession started off again. Sailors pulled the gun carriage past the Guildhall, through Park Street and entered the castle grounds through the Cambridge Gate, and thence to St. George's Chapel where the funeral service was held.

Since that time the honour of pulling the monarch's gun carriage to the funeral has always gone to the Royal Navy. After the service the coffin was taken to the Albert Memorial Chapel where it rested until Monday.

3rd February As the day was Sunday, no further progress could be made with the funeral, though rehearsals were held during the night.

4th February A limited number of members of the public were allowed to watch the procession pass as it turned into the Long Walk on its way to Frogmore. Horses from the Royal Artillery were used to pull the gun carriage until it reached the beautiful Royal Mausoleum where Queen Victoria was laid beside her beloved Albert who had been placed there in 1869.

Chapter 5 1901-2000

Westward to the World Wide Web

When Queen Victoria died during the first few days of the new century Windsor was still a small town clustered around the castle. During her reign it had grown and modernised but no Victorian could have imagined the changes that would take place in the next hundred years.

In 1901 Clewer Without, which included Dedworth, was a separate civil parish with its own services including a police station at the corner of Clarence Road and Parsonage Lane. In 1904, Windsor tried to take over Clewer. The inhabitants resisted and won their freedom, but in 1920 Clewer and Dedworth became part of Windsor without a fight. Windsor needed this rural land to expand and slowly the farms to the west of the castle were sold and turned into housing estates. In the 1920s Vale Farm was purchased to build council houses and in the 1930s Church Farm land was earmarked for rehousing those left homeless by slum clearance schemes. In the 1940s prefabs were built even further west by German prisoners of war. In the 1950s the first houses of a huge private development were built to the west of Smith's Lane, Dedworth. This scheme carried on in the 1960s with houses backing on to the boundary of Bray at Willows Path. Windsor was bursting at the seams. Bounded to the north by the river, to the east and south by the Great Park, it must have been a great relief to the planners when in 1974 Windsor merged with Maidenhead to become the Royal Borough of Windsor and Maidenhead, and land in Bray became available.

The movement has not been all in the same direction. In the fifties Old Windsor began to grow and new housing estates meant that mains drainage was at last laid on. Some of the fine houses in the village have been turned into flats and the old village school, St Peter's, has been enlarged and a second school, Kings Court, was built in the sixties.

In 1982 Dedworth became an ecclesiastical parish in its own right, having previously been part of either Windsor or Clewer. The area of the new parish included land that had been in Clewer parish and Bray. Only thirty years earlier, Dedworth did not even have pavements - it was not the sort of place that 'decent' people went to. Now, everyone goes there to visit Tesco.

The administration of the town moved in 1974 from the Kipling Building in Alma Road to Maidenhead Town Hall. The marriage of the two towns has been a somewhat uneasy relationship. Historically, quite different factors affected the development of Windsor and Maidenhead. Public transport links between the two towns have always been poor. Each town has its own newspapers, and different TV companies supply local news, with the result that there is a lack of understanding of local issues by residents.

Windsor no longer exists as a separate administrative unit in several other ways. The Magistrates Court was closed after 560 years and cases are now heard in Slough or Bracknell. Many of the hospital services, for which our Edwardian forebears fought so hard, have been transferred to Wexham Park Hospital or to Heatherwood. Although some departments remain at the King Edward VII building, there is no longer an Accident and Emergency department in the town. Bus services now centre on the Brunel bus station at Slough rather than Windsor. We are just a small part of the Thames Valley Police area. Windsor and Maidenhead College of Further Education merged with Langley College to become East Berkshire College, and it is thought sufficient to offer some courses at one location only.

A hundred years ago the traders in Windsor were local businesses. In the year 2000, although the number of shops and other firms offering employment has grown considerably, they are now run by multiples. At ground level the scene is the same as in any other town in the country but a glance upwards to the first floor reminds us of the earlier days. There are timber-framed buildings and a nineteenth century photographer's studio among the quaint mix of first floor architecture.

The coming of the railways in the nineteenth century revolutionised transport and in the twentieth century real horsepower has been superseded by the motor vehicle, with the result that our roads are choked with cars, huge lorries and coaches. We see very few horses on our roads and they are ridden either by soldiers training for ceremonial occasions or hobby riders, though the Royal Windsor Horse Show, the Driving Championships and the racecourse ensure that we see more horses than most towns.

The presence of the Royal Family in the town, and the existence of television, means that the rest of the world is more aware of Windsor than it was in the past. The Queen celebrated her Silver Jubilee during 1977, the same year as the town celebrated its sepcentenary. She chose Windsor to light the beacon that started a chain across the whole country, and television viewers were there to watch. The fire that burned at the castle for a whole day in 1992 was seen in every country. Royal children have married at St George's Chapel before but they did not have live television cameras watching as Prince Edward did in 1999. Today Windsor seems to belong to the whole world rather than its inhabitants.

In many towns churches are being de-consecrated, and used for secular purposes, even housing. This has not happened yet in Windsor, though the position of some of them is under review. St John's Parish Church, whilst continuing to be used for civic services, has been adapted for use as a concert venue. Other churches in the town centre, both Anglican and Non-conformist, whilst retaining their religious functions have, by the provision of meeting rooms and kitchens, sought to meet the daily needs of the local community. This trend is also evident at Old Windsor and at Dedworth where the rebuilt All Saints' Church, and three other churches built there in the last fifty years to meet the needs of the rapidly growing population, all offer community facilities.

But one religious organisation is closing - the Convent. A hundred years ago Clewer was a well-known place in some of the remoter parts of the world because the nuns from the Convent of St John the Baptist were running schools, hospitals and orphanages. This was a massive organisation run by intrepid nuns who went from Hatch Lane to minister to the poor in this country and the remotest parts of the British Empire. The demise of the Empire and the rise of the health service and council-run social services have meant that there is less call for their work. The last half century has seen their numbers getting smaller, and in the year 2000 they announced that they were packing up and leaving. The buildings are up for sale.

There have been many other changes, notably the removal of the slums. Areas of the town such as Grove Road, that were once condemned as slums, have been modernised and some are quite fashionable. The Workhouse at Old Windsor became a hospital and has now has been turned into desirable flats. Other problem areas have been turned into car parks. We no longer get regular epidemics of disease, and cures are available for some of those that would have been fatal in the past. Any one who is really poor can call on the social services for help. Working people do get salaries they can live on, and health care is available free. The flood relief scheme is under way and so regular flooding may also be a thing of the past. Most of the organisations that have opened in the twentieth century are for leisure pursuits, like the Arts Centre and Athletics Club. Communication is world wide and we can benefit from the international exchange of information. The Royal Borough of Windsor and Maidenhead designed their own website in 2000 so that residents and non-residents can get instant access to information about council decisions.

Many of the problems and miseries of the nineteenth century are no longer the main issues for local government. We are part of a larger community.

Pamela Marson

Proclamation of His Most Gracious Majesty King Edward VII.

BOROUGH OF NEW WINDSOR.

MONDAY, JANUARY 28th, 1901.

Assemble at the Guildhall at 11.30 a.m. Procession will leave the Guildhall at 12 o'clock and proceed to the Statute on Castle Hill.

ORDER OF PROCESSION.

HERALDS.
MACE BEARER.
THE MAYOR (Walter P. Reavell, Esq., J.P.), and the ALDERMEN,
COUNCILLORS, and OFFICAILS of the Borough.
THE JUSTICES OF THE PEACE FOR THE BOROUGH AND CLERK.
THE JUSTICES OF THE PEACE FOR THE WINDSOR DIVISION OF THE
COUNTY OF BERKS.
THE CLERGY AND MINISTERS.
REPRESENTATIVES OF LOCAL AUTHORITIES.
REPRESENTATIVES OF PUBLIC SCHOOLS.

AT THE STATUE—

FANFARE OF TRUMPETS.
The Proclamation will be read by THE RIGHT WORSHIPFUL THE MAYOR.
FANFARE OF TRUMPETS.
NATIONAL ANTHEM (Band of the 1st Life Guards, by kind permission of Colonel Miles.)

The Procession will then proceed to Henry VIII.'s Gateway, where the Dean and Canons of St. George's, Military Knights, and Officials will receive the Mayor.
FANFARE OF TRUMPETS.
THE PROCLAMATION.
FANFARE.
NATIONAL ANTHEM.

The Procession will proceed to the Eton side of the Windsor Bridge, where the Mayor will be received by the Provost and Fellows of Eton College, and the Chairman and Members of the Eton Urban District Council and Officials.
FANFARE OF TRUMPETS.
THE PROCLAMATION.
FANFARE.
NATIONAL ANTHEM.

Return to the Guildhall.

"God Save the King."

WALTER P. REAVELL,
Mayor.

The Mayors leaflet publicising arrangements for the proclamation of King Edward VII.

1902   There was an increase in the numbers attending the infirmary. As a result it was proposed to build on a different site. Bachelors' Acre was suggested and all that was necessary was a vote in favour at the council meeting. However, Sir Joseph Devereaux objected. The mayor said, "Pardon me, Sir Joseph, it is too late to go into that now". "I don't think so," said Sir Joseph. Alderman Clarke then produced photographs of the narrow passages onto the Acre and claimed that it was the only playground that some poor children had. Once again the Acre was saved, and not for the last time.
Sir Arthur Rollit and his wife, the Duchess of Sutherland, bought Surly Hall at Dedworth, and pulled it down.

1904   There was an official enquiry into the reluctance of Clewer Without Parish Council to be included in the Borough of New Windsor. The inspector decided that the services provided by Clewer Without were efficient and it remained independent. On 8th May there was a service at St Andrew's Parish Church to give thanks for their safe deliverance.
Electricity reached Old Windsor.
The statue of Prince Christian Victor, by W. Gosgombe John, with a canopy by AY Nutt was unveiled in its present position near the bottom of the Hundred Steps.
The premises of Rodgers & Denyer, Windsor's largest department store, were destroyed by fire.

1905   *18th July* **Windsor's First Buses** The first regular motor omnibus service to Windsor started. It was run by Great Western Railway from Slough Station to Windsor Central Station and took just 15 minutes.
William Maxwell opened a grocer's shop in Alexandra Road. His son, James, then 18 months old, was to spend his whole life at the shop, retiring in 1983.
The foundation stone for a new municipal building was laid by Sir William Shipley in St Leonard's Road. Its function had not been decided (see 1907).
Part of this building is now Windsor Arts Centre.

Peascod Street in 1905

Peascod Street 1906

1906 St Stephen's Senior Girls School moved to newly built premises in Vansittart Road. It was known previously as the Intermediate or Upper Grade School for Girls.

1907 *28th February* Sir Francis Tress Barry died.
The King gave permission for the new hospital to be called King Edward VII Hospital and Dispensary for Windsor, Eton and District. Sir William Shipley had raised a large amount of money.
The King held a garden party at the castle and invited many of the famous men and women of the day, including Thomas Hardy, Mark Twain, the actress Ellen Terry, actor-manager Sir Herbert Beerbohm Tree, and the singers Dame Nellie Melba and Clara Butt. As a result Windsor suffered its first motor traffic jam.
The new municipal building in St Leonard's Road opened as a police station, magistrates' court and fire station.

1908 *22nd June* A commemoration stone was laid at the new hospital site by the King, accompanied by the Queen and Prince and Princess Christian.
18th February Theatre Royal, in Thames Street, was destroyed by fire.
By special request of the King the Olympic marathon started at the castle.
The newly enlarged Church of St Agnes Spital was dedicated by the Bishop of Reading, the Rt Revd James Leslie Randall.
Windsor County Boys School opened in Church House by Holy Trinity Church.
The first scout troop was started in Windsor, but was short-lived.

1909 *17th March* The new hospital received its first patients. There were 50 beds.
King Edward's Ward was for men, Queen Alexandra's Ward was for women and Helena Ward for children. The accident and emergency ward was called Barry Ward (after Sir Francis Tress Barry) and Dr Hathaway organised a horse ambulance for these cases.

1909   Windsor Swimming Club was formed.
cont.   The 1st Windsor Scouts was formed by St John's Church and 2nd Windsors by the Congregational Church in William Street.

1910   *11th May*   George V was proclaimed King next to the statue of Queen Victoria by the mayor, Frederick Dyson. The mayor was then received at the castle and on the Eton side of Windsor Bridge.
         18th August   Clewer Mill was burned down.

The Old Mill

Mills anciently belonged to the Lord of the Manor and tenants were permitted to grind only at the lord's mill. At the time of the Domesday survey in 1086 **Clewer Mill** was valued at ten shillings as compared with the two mills at Eton which were each worth twice that amount. The mill, a water driven corn mill, stood on the banks of the mill stream which was an arm of the Thames or an artificial channel. It appears to have been continuously in operation from the time of domesday until 1910 when, as recorded by AY Nutt, it was burnt down. Fire seems to have been a frequent hazard at the mill. An illustrated article about Clewer Mill in the 1781 *Westminster Magazine* states that before its destruction by fire 'the interior machinery of the mill was extremely curious and singular, and drew the attention of the King and many of the nobility to visit it'. In the nineteenth century, the Aldridge family and later the Vidler family were corn millers at Clewer. Thomas Aldridge, son of the proprietor, gave evidence at the inquest of John Brackenbury, who had died in an accident at the mill in 1815. John Webb Aldridge, aged 64, employed 14 men at the mill in 1851 and there was a resident foreman miller. The mill was rebuilt in the 1860s soon after John and George Vidler, millers and farmers, took over. John Vidler's son, John Edmund Vidler, was a miller and the family business continued until the mill ceased operation. It is not known whether the mill was rebuilt after the 1910 fire but by then the property was known as 'The Old Mill House'.

Joyce Sampson

      A new building was provided at the hospital for pathology.
      The Goswells was purchased by the National Trust to preserve the view of the castle from the river.
      The 3rd Windsor Scouts was formed at Clewer St Stephen's Church, the 4th Windsors at Holy Trinity Church and 5th Windsors at Clewer St Andrew's.

1911   *9th September*   The first airmail delivery in the UK took place in Windsor. Pilot Gustave Hammell landed in Shaw Farm meadow with letters including one for the Windsor postmaster.
         Mayor Knighted   Frederick Dyson, the mayor, was publicly knighted as the new King George V entered Windsor after his coronation.
         England's first police dog, 'Nigger', was presented to Clewer New Town Police by Sir Theodore Brinkman.

1911   Imperial Service College was formed from a number of private schools
cont.   including St Mark's School. The college was to occupy a number of buildings
       in the Alma Road area of Windsor until 1942.
       The first major honour won by Windsor and Eton Football Club was the Berks
       and Bucks Senior Cup in the 1910/11 season. They had played in the final in 1908.

1912   The statue of King Edward VII by Countess Feodora Gleichen was unveiled
       at the hospital. £5000 was given by Mrs. Elliman for a female surgical ward.
       Following the Titanic disaster the body of one of the victims, Owen Allum,
       was buried in Clewer Churchyard. He was only 17 years old.

1914   *1st June* Suffragettes set fire to the Willows at Dedworth, home of the anti-
       suffrage MP Roger Eykyn.
       15th August The Life Guards left Windsor for the front a few days after the
       declaration of the First World War (known at the time as the Great War).
       The outbreak of war and an increasing population meant more work for the
       hospital. Wounded servicemen were patients.

1915   *9th August* A public telephone call office was built into Dedworth post office,
       which was on the north side of Dedworth Road, next to the Queen public
       house.
       1st November Windsor resident Oliver Brooks was awarded a VC for
       conspicuous bravery near Loos. He led a party under fire and regained 200
       yards that had just been lost.

1916   Victoria Barracks was extended over Love Lane.

1917   *28th April* At the request of the mayor, Queen Mary with Prince George
       (later Duke of Kent), Prince Henry (later Duke of Gloucester) and Princess
       Mary drove through the town in a coach to boost morale at a low point in the
       war. Church bells were rung and the streets decorated with the flags of the
       allies. The Queen went to the hospital where wounded soldiers were laid out
       in cots on the grass.
       17th July The Royal Family adopted the name Windsor replacing the
       German Saxe-Coburg-Gotha.
       Squire Foster of Clewer Manor died aged 93.
       HMS Windsor was launched. It was a W class destroyer and was supported
       by the town.
       Medical staff at the hospital were called into the Royal Army Medical Corps.
       Archaeological excavations began at Bears Rails, Old Windsor, because it
       was thought to be the site of the Anglo-Saxon palace. Nothing significant was
       found.

1917 Barclays Bank set up a local head office in the Windsor Branch, which is still
cont. on the corner of High Street and Peascod Street, though the local head office
moved out to a site by the river in 1973.

FJ Lane, builders and decorators, opened in the premises in Temple Road that
they still occupy in 2000.

1918 *11th November* **The Great War is Over** Samuel Maun, (Station master at
Windsor Great Western Station from 1903-1925) had started the 8.47am train
and returned to his office to find Princess Alice at the door. "I have some
news for you" she said. "The armistice was signed in a railway coach at 6
am, but it is not to be made known until 11am. I was sure you would like to
know, so don't tell anyone until then."

During the Great War about 600 men from the Windsor area were killed
including four sons of John and Jane Wilkins of Vine Cottage, Clewer New
Town.

Thirteen Times Mayor of Windsor!

William Carter (1848-1932) was born in Marlow and educated
there at the elementary school which he left when he was 12 years
old. His first job was as a painter and decorator but he did not like
the work and left after a few months. He did learn to glaze windows
and paint a room and he said that the knowledge came in handy.
He worked for two years as a gardener in Marlow and then worked
for Sir George Du Pre in Beaconsfield, again as a gardener. He
earned twelve shillings a week and lived in a bothy. It was here
that he met his wife, who worked in the house. They married in
Beaconsfield in 1871. William Carter's fourth job was a change of
direction for him, as it was with the Prudential Insurance Company
in the Marlow district. Promotion brought him to Windsor where
he decided to stay despite further offers of promotion in Reading
and London. He retired at the age limit of 60 years in 1908. He was first elected to Windsor Borough
Council in November 1902 and was made an Alderman in 1922. He was mayor of Windsor thirteen
times between 1908 and 1927 including the whole of the first world war. He was knighted for
services to the town and created a Freeman of Windsor in 1925, when he was presented with a
grandfather clock together with an illuminated address, signed by Princess Alice of Athlone among
others. When he and his wife celebrated their diamond wedding in 1931 congratulations were
received from The King, Queen and Prince of Wales. He died in October 1932 at his home, Suffolk
Lodge, in Bolton Road aged 84, and left the council a valuable collection of silver plate.

Colin Gray

1918 The problems of disabled soldiers were realised at the hospital and an
cont. orthopaedic treatment room was constructed which ultimately served as the
physiotherapy department. A motor ambulance was bought to replace the
horse-drawn ambulance that had operated for ten years.

Charles Daniel rented 120 Peascod Street from the mayor, Sir J. Soundy, and
opened a draper's shop which he named WJ Daniel & Co after his father,
who already had a shop in Ealing. In 2000 Daniels, now much enlarged, is a
prominent department store.

1919 The Registration of Nurses Act became law and arrangements were made to
prepare the probationer nurses at King Edward VII Hospital to become State
Registered Nurses.
The first council house in Windsor was built in Clewer Avenue.
A disabled ex-service man was refused a licence for the Queen public house
at Dedworth, by the Superintendent of Police, because he had lost an arm
during the war and the house could only be controlled by an able-bodied man.
Caleys was sold to Harry Gordon Selfridge of Selfridges.
17th November Midland Bank opened at 25 High Street, Windsor. The first
manager was JM Burns who remained in the post until 1934. The branch is
still there but the bank has merged with HSBC.

1920 *4th May* Clewer Without was included in the Municipal Borough of Windsor
under an extension order, only sixteen years after an official enquiry had
allowed the parish to remain independent.
St Stephen's College for the daughters of the gentry and the clergy, which had
50 boarders, moved to Folkestone.
22nd September Windsor County Girls' School opened at Elmfield in Kings
Road with 46 pupils aged 10 and over.
The Fifield Mission came under the care of the Windsor Free Church Council.
The area covered by the Mission included Dedworth.
Windsorian Coaches was started by Reg Try.
A tank arrived at Bachelors' Acre with great ceremony. It was a gift from
the War Department for the substantial amount of money collected for the
war effort by Windsorians.

1921 *January* King Edward VII Gateway was opened and the bust of the King
over it was unveiled by Princess Alice, Countess of Athlone. The gateway is
still at the top of a flight of stairs which leads from Thames Street to the
Alexandra Gardens and the riverside. The passage was donated to the people
of Windsor by Sir Jesse Boot when his Boots store on the site was rebuilt. It
is still known as Boots Passage, though Boots store is now in Peascod Street.

A Windsorian to his fingertips

Born at Racecourse Cottage, Maidenhead Road, the third generation of the Try family to be born in Clewer, **Reginald Aden Robert Try** was educated at St Stephen's School in Trinity Place and Windsor Grammar School. He worked briefly for Sir Dhunjibhoy Bomanji at The Willows, and for the Electric Light Co, which was behind Creaks outfitters. He also collected and delivered film tins to the Regal Cinema in Peascod Street. After serving in the Air Training Corps, he used his demob money to buy a World War One ambulance from the Slough 'dump' and he and his brother fitted it out as a bus in a garage behind the White Hart Hotel. Racing to be first ensured him of his passengers and many were ferried from the Guildhall to Ascot on race days. From humble beginnings, through charabanc days the fleet grew to eighteen Windsorian Coaches. They took thousands on holiday tours and days by the sea and even took the royal family to a lunch party at Bray.

During World War II RegTry delivered parcels to pensioners as a Rotarian, was on bomb watch as a special constable, and as a councillor helped to organise the fundraising 'Salute the Soldiers' campaign, placing a giant thermometer on the castle walls. When he purchased St Leonard's Hill he inherited the trusteeship of Clewer Green School. He also set up travel agencies in Slough and Windsor and travelled world-wide. A charming gentleman, he was the self-appointed ambassador for his beloved Windsor.

Valerie Batt-Rawden

Windsor Parish Church Bellringers on their annual outing in 1921
in Reg Try's first Windsorian Coach.

119

1921
cont.
    Artefacts from the Royal Albert Institute Museum were sent to Hull Museum as the rooms were needed for recreational facilities for wounded soldiers. Hull sold some items to the Victoria and Albert Museum and exchanged others for East Yorkshire examples with the Ashmolean Museum at Oxford.

    Windsor Rugby Club was revived, using pitches in the Home Park

    The widow of Squire Foster died and Clewer Manor was sold to Imperial Service College as a junior department.

    The British Legion (now the Royal British Legion) Men's Section Windsor Branch was formed. The first chairman was Major Carteret-Carey.

1922
    King George V allowed Windsor to be called a Royal Borough to regularise a situation that already existed, as many people were already using the word Royal to describe the borough. Unfortunately no-one in the borough recorded the fact in the council minutes. From this year the new mayor was always elected as Mayor of this Royal and Ancient Borough, but no other action was taken.

    A new telephone exchange was built on Bachelors' Acre. The previous one on Datchet Road was closed.

    Windsor Bowls Club was formed from a general sports club.

    The British Legion (now Royal British Legion) Women's Section Windsor Branch was formed.

The Benevolent Parsee

Sir Dhunjibhoy Bomanji lived in The Willows on the Thames riverside, Windsor, from 1922 until his death in Bombay in 1937. He was a Parsee and a successful businessman amongst the Bombay shipping suppliers. His wife, Lady Frainy, was a beautiful, talented and educated woman who was known as 'the Rose of Poona' and assisted him in his many works of charity. Well known in Windsor for his grand life-style (a fleet of pale blue Rolls Royces, a beautiful launch on the river and lavish parties with his Royal friends) he was also generous to many good causes including the King Edward VII Hospital. As a friend of Earl Haig he befriended ex-servicemen and contributed £5000 to the Ex-Servicemen's Club in St Leonard's Road. During the war The Willows was bombed and the family moved to Harrogate where Lady Frainy Bomanji was made a Freeman of the City in the 1980s.

Sheila Rooney

1923   Following the discovery of insulin treatment for diabetes, King Edward VII Hospital became one of the first provincial hospitals to take a special interest in this development. A nurses' hostel was built at the south-east corner of the hospital. There were 30 bedrooms. The British Red Cross Society gave £1000 and Sir Dhunjibhoy Bomanji gave £5000.

1924   *28th April* The King and Queen made a train journey from Windsor and Eton Station to Swindon and back.

1926   The Imperial Coach service was started by the Moore family in Firs Avenue.
Lady Barry, widow of Sir Francis Tress Barry, died, and their home, St Leonard's Hill, was partially demolished by the trustees.
St Leonard's water tower was built.
The Royal Albert Laundry's premises in Bourne Avenue went up in flames.
The Token House opened in Windsor High Street.
A car park and public lavatories, including a bath house, were built in River Street, replacing the slums that had been demolished. It was the first car park in Windsor.
The council began negotiations to buy Vale Farm at Dedworth with the intention of building public housing.

1927   King George wing was built at King Edward VII Hospital.
Permission was granted to build 144 houses on the Vale Farm site.
The tin chapel, by Helen Cottages in Dedworth Road, came under the control of the three non-conformist churches in Windsor having been under the control of the Fifield Mission.

1928   *24th April* Fire at the hospital resulted in the loss of Alexandra and Edward wards. Under the leadership of Sir James Gomer Berry (later Lord Kemsley) the wards were rebuilt rapidly with the addition of a further storey named Queen Mary Ward. Open balconies were provided at the end of each ward.

1929   *16th January* JW Hambidge became full-time town clerk. Until this time the work had been carried out by private firms of solicitors.
A new nurses' home was built in memory of Lady Gomer Berry. This freed the eastern wing to be used by patients. An extension over George V Ward was also provided and financed by Sir Edward Stern, a wealthy banker of Carlton House Terrace, Slough.

1930   *January* 500 trees were blown down in Windsor, by gales.
Trevelyan School was opened by Rt Hon. Sir Charles Trevelyan Bt MP, President of the Board of Education.

1930   The old infirmary building in Bachelors' Acre was sold to the Windsor Liberal
cont.   Club. The money was used to purchase Ewhurst House and nearly one acre
        of land. The pathology department was allocated most of the ground floor.
        The old pathology building at the west end of the hospital was converted into
        the hospital chapel.
        Windsor Ladies Gymnastics Club closed after 21 years because ladies were
        playing outdoor games more.

        The Southern Railway spent £366,000 electrifying the line between Windsor
        and Waterloo.
        The Windsor Cinema in Peascod Street changed its name to the Regal and
        converted to showing talkies instead of silent films.

1931   King Edward Horse Hall was built by Imperial Service College as their main hall.
        Money was provided by the King Edward VII's Horse Regiment Endowment Fund.
        Small Earthquake A small earthquake woke Windsor residents in the middle of
        the night on 7th June.

Earning a living

Hard though it was to earn a living in Windsor in the mid-thirties, there was a small group of local people who did manage to find casual work.

The Pavement Artist - Every Saturday outside Barclays Bank at the top of Peascod Street a screever would transform the grey pavement slabs into attractive and colourful drawings. Many coloured chalks would be used to achieve the final result. He would be seated there with a small container in which passers-by might feel inclined to drop a few pence.

The Flower Sellers - Outside the Guildhall beside the fountain, a man and his wife could be seen throughout the week with containers laden with every variety of flowers in season. Their displays were as attractive as a rainbow and customers were drawn to purchase from the scene before their eyes.

The Fish Seller - At the rear of the Guildhall on Saturday evenings a small market stall could be seen with trays of small seasonal shell fish such as whelks, winkles and cockles, which were served on circular four inch plates. The stall was brightly lit by an overhead gas jet, and nearby the proprietor, wearing a crisp white apron was ready to serve.

The Post Card Sellers - Daily a few men would stand on Castle Hill with packets of sepia picture postcards of the Castle and Eton College, which they sold to visitors many of whom were foreign. The postcards were purchased from a very well-known shop in St Leonard's Road. The men were not allowed to put a foot on the pavement.

The Carpet Beater - There used to be a man of very slight stature who made a living beating carpets from large houses in the town. He pushed them on a handcart to an area of grass in Claremont Road, and there he beat them with a wicker carpet beater.

Ellen Dollery

1932   London Passenger Transport Board opened a bus garage opposite the King Edward VII Hospital.

The Rotary Club of Windsor and Eton was invested with its charter. The first president was the Dean of Windsor.

Two motor refuse-collecting wagons replaced the former horse-drawn vehicles.

1933   *April* Marks and Spencer opened a shop on part of their present site.

A squash club was opened in Brook Street.

Soldiers go by Coach The Foot Guards abandoned the practice of marching to London from Windsor in favour of using motor coaches.

St Leonard's was bought by Mrs Horace Dodge, who rebuilt the house.

Windsor Free Library was opened at the old British School in Victoria Street.

1934   The council began negotiations to buy Church Farm at Dedworth, in order to erect 66 houses for people whose houses were being demolished in slum clearance schemes in central Windsor.

1935   Windsor celebrated the Silver Jubilee of King George V and Queen Mary.

1936   *20th January* King George V died and was succeeded by his eldest son Edward VIII.

It was at the time of the funeral of King George V that cars were parked on Bachelors' Acre for the first time. This became a regular habit.

8th October Bell Farm Estate, the home of Major Tennant was sold. The estate extended from Clewer Hill Road to Dedworth Road. The site was developed by Varney's and the bungalows that were built there were considered to be the beginning of 'West Windsor'. One of the roads was named Bell View, the others included St Andrew's Crescent.

11th December **The Abdication** Edward VIII abdicated, making his famous speech from Windsor Castle. He was succeeded by his brother, Albert, who took the name George VI.

1937   Windsor Royal Gaslight Company became part of the South-Eastern Gas Corporation.

King George V Memorial was built at the corner of Datchet Road. It was designed by Edmund Lutyens and unveiled by King George VI whose coronation took place on 12th May.

Mrs Carteret-Carey was elected Windsor's first woman mayor.

1938   *25th February* The short-lived Royalty Cinema closed and reopened as The Theatre Royal on 21st March. John Counsell produced *Clive of India*.

Part of the Home Park was handed over to Windsor Council.

1938
cont.

St Leonard's was occupied by the American Ambassador, Joseph Kennedy.
Windsor Boys School moved to the present site in Maidenhead Road.
August Two parties of Germans were made welcome in the town. Ex-servicemen viewed the inside of the castle, and sixteen leaders of the Hitler Youth Movement were the guests of the mayor, Mrs Carteret-Carey, who showed them the east terrace of the castle. They expressed surprise that a woman could become mayor.

Meanwhile, preparations were made in case of war. Air-raid wardens were appointed and given training on how to pass through a 'gas chamber'. Training exercises in case of bombing were undertaken and sirens were tested.

Offers were made of cellars for shelters including those at the Victoria Laundry which was on the former site of Burges Brewery.

1939

January Windsor County Boys' School's new building was officially opened by the Earl of Athlone and Princess Alice.

1st September A hundred patients were evacuated from St Bartholomew's Hospital in London to King Edward VII hospital, just two days before the outbreak of the second World War. The hospital was included in the Emergency Medical Service and made the headquarters of the pathological services in the sector.

Thousands of evacuees were received at Windsor station. 1000 beds were collected from Leeds. School hours were shortened so that evacuees could share school premises and teachers.

Windsor Baptists took responsibility for the Fifield Mission, at the tin Chapel in Dedworth Road.

1940

13th May HMS Windsor evacuated the Dutch Government from Holland
23/24th May HMS Windsor evacuated troops from France.
May Raymond South was one of those who enrolled at the police station in St Leonard's Road for the Home Guard. He was soon filling bags with earth to create a barricade along Smith's Lane to resist a German advance from the direction of Bray (while at Bray they were preparing to resist a German advance from the direction of Windsor).

A Messerschmitt ME 109 aircraft crashed behind Stag Meadow. The Princesses Elizabeth and Margaret were taken to see it.

The tank on Bachelors' Acre was scrapped to help the war effort.

The Thames was frozen over. Skaters were seen on the Thames.

1941

Caleys becomes part of John Lewis Caleys was sold to the John Lewis Partnership in whose ownership it remains in the year 2000.

Windsor citizens raised £374,968 in War Weapon Week in May.

1941
Cont.
A British Restaurant was opened at 127 Peascod Street, formerly Kirkbys Bakery. These restaurants were sponsored by the Ministry of Food, for those who could not go home to lunch. At a time of severe food rationing, coupons were not required to buy meals.

1942
The ruins of St Leonard's Hill and the land attached were bought by Reg Try. The deer in Windsor Great Park were removed to Balmoral.
Imperial Service College merged with Haileybury School. The boys transferred to Haileybury's premises near Hertford, and the buildings were used by the War Department.

1943
The first Windsor Horse Show was held in May. The Royal Windsor Horse Show Club was formed in November.
The council bought Imperial Service College's Kipling Building for £37,000. The War Office was using the building and the borough did not expect to gain possession until after the war.
Elm Trees in the Long Walk were felled because they were in a diseased state and horse chestnut and plane trees planted in their place the following year.

1944
1st July A German flying bomb fell in Dedworth demolishing the chimney of the dust destructor and damaging many houses in Kenton's Lane. There was damage as far away as Vale Road. Another V1 demolished the Bells of Ouseley at Old Windsor and a mother and her daughter were killed.

Kentons Lane, Dedworth in the mid-1930s. On the right is the dust destructor chimney that was demolished by the V1 bomb

15th September Windsor's Streets were illuminated for the first time for five years. Clewer St Stephen's Senior Girls School was re-named Princess Margaret Rose School when Princess Margaret became patron.

1945   *19th January* The Minister of Health approved the building of temporary bungalows on 19.19 acres of land at Wolf Lane, Dedworth. Commonly known as prefabs, they were built by German prisoners of war, who had an armed guard. The prisoners were paid three farthings an hour for the work, an amount agreed by the Geneva Convention. The men did not mind, as it was more interesting than being in a prison camp.

8th May VE Day **Victory in Europe**. Flags appeared in houses and shops, and there were celebrations on Bachelors' Acre.

May The British Restaurant closed.

15th August VJ Day **Victory in Japan.**

6th October Windsor began a week of thanksgiving.

9th November Sixteen Labour members were elected to the council, the largest number ever, including Raymond and Marjorie South.

Housing for the Destitute becomes a Hospital

The Union Workhouse at Old Windsor was built in 1840 to cater for the needs of the destitute and aged of Windsor, Old Windsor, Sunningdale and Sunninghill. It was presided over by a master and mistress and housed up to 200 inmates when fully occupied. Those able to work were expected to carry out jobs in the buildings and adjacent gardens and, as far as one can judge from records, food included vegetables and fruit grown there. The children were at one time taught by a resident teacher, but later they were sent to nearby St Peter's School. In 1945 the workhouse became part of King Edward VII Hospital and in 1998 it was converted into private housing.

Margaret Gilson

1946   *18th January* Windsor Civic Society constituted.

Keelers optical firm started at Sefton Lawn, Clewer Hill Road.

Windsor elected its first Labour Mayor, Alderman Frederick Fuzzens.

The council decided to apply to become a Royal Borough. Extensive research was done into the history of the borough so that a different coat of arms could be incorporated into the new insignia. However, when the council wrote to the Home Secretary on the matter, he wrote back and told them that they were already a Royal Borough (see 1922). The name of the borough was officially changed to The Royal Borough of New Windsor.

1947   *March* Extensive floods followed a long, very cold winter. The water was some six feet above normal at Windsor Bridge. Flood mail was delivered to upstairs rooms on a pole with a bulldog clip.

Princess Elizabeth received the Freedom of Windsor.

Windsor Baptists bought a site in Smiths Lane where they planned to build a new Church.

1947 Brigidine School opened at Queensmead.
cont. Control of the police was transferred from the town to Berkshire County
Council.
HMS Windsor was scrapped.
Further Education in Windsor was organised at many different sites by
Windsor Technical Institute.

Floods at the corner of Vale Road and Buckland Crescent

1948 *March* The hottest March on record brought water shortages just one year
after the flooding.
5th July King Edward VII Hospital was incorporated into the new National
Health Service and became one of the hospitals under the administration of
the Windsor Group Hospital Management Committee.
30th July Gordon Wrigley of Windsor Harriers carried the Olympic flame
through Windsor Great Park to Eton Bridge on its way to Wembley.
November A 21-gun salute in the Long Walk initiated by Alderman Fred
Fuzzens was fired to celebrate the birth of a son, Charles, to Princess
Elizabeth and Prince Philip on 14th November. The bells of the Curfew Tower
were heard across the town in celebration.
The Union Workhouse at Old Windsor was taken over by King Edward VII
Hospital at Windsor.

1949   *6th April* An experimental double decker 'Greenline' coach started making
        two daily trips from Windsor to Tunbridge Wells. It was claimed to be the
        most advanced passenger road vehicle in the world.
        North Thames Gas Board took over the South-Eastern Gas Corporation.
        'Bygone Windsor' Exhibition organised by Windsor and Eton Society, and opened
        by Sir Owen Morshead, was held at Windsor Guildhall. This exhibition was the
        inspiration for the Guildhall Exhibition which was opened two years later.
        The Victoria Laundry (Windsor) Ltd sued Newman Industries Ltd because
        the boiler that Newmans supplied arrived late and as a result Victoria Laundry
        was not awarded a valuable contract they had been expecting. The verdict is
        now case law and is still studied by law students. [The laundry was awarded
        compensation for the work they could not do because of the late arrival of the
        boiler but were not awarded any compensation for the loss of the contract.]
        Windsor and Eton Athletic Club formed.

1950   A list of buildings in Windsor which should be preserved was compiled and
        published. They became official 'listed buildings' and should not be
        demolishedor altered without permission.
        Dysons installed a clock in the pavement outside their shop at 9 Thames
        Street. This became one of the sights that visitors to the town had to see, and
        Dysons became known as 'The Firm with the Clock in the Pavement'.
        A restoration programme began at the Guildhall in preparation for the Festival
        of Britain in 1951.
        The Royal Albert Institute building was let for educational purposes.
        Kipling Building became the administrative centre of the borough, replacing
        the Guildhall.

1951   An important archaeological excavation took place near Old Windsor Church,
        which revealed the site of the original Saxon Windsor. The excavations were
        led by Brian Hope-Taylor and continued until 1957.

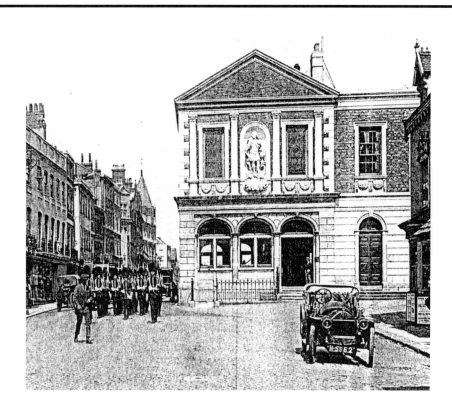

Windsor Guildhall before the 1951 refurbishment

The present Guildhall was built 1687-1690 and for nearly three hundred years it was the civic heart of the Borough of New Windsor - its town hall and market place. Here the town council met and held its courts of justice and administration. The open area beneath the council chamber was used as a corn exchange and the ground floor area of the extension built in 1829 was used for a meat and poultry market. The Guildhall was also the venue for social events - balls and banquets, exhibitions, concerts and public meetings of all kinds. Here parliamentary elections took place, noisy unruly affairs when voting was in public. For many years it also housed the borough archives in a walk-in strong-room, and from 1951 to 1983 it was the home of the town museum.

Judith Hunter

1951
cont.

The Guildhall restoration was completed including the removal of the
wood and glass screens. The Guildhall Exhibition of Windsor Local History
was opened by Princess Elizabeth to coincide with the Festival of Britain.
The curator was Maitland Underhill.
First Windsor Championship Dog Show was held.
Windsor Round Table and Windsor Forest Bowmen were founded.

1952

Elizabeth II was proclaimed Queen on the death of her father, King George
VI. The proclamation was made at Queen Victoria's Statue.
Work began on the construction of a primary school on the present site of
Dedworth First School. It was then known as Dedworth Infants School.
6th August Windsor District Trefoil Guild was registered. The first meeting
was held at the British School.
Old Windsor Gospel Hall became a Methodist Church.
Land in Claremont Road was sold to Berkshire County Council to build East
Berkshire College, the new permanent home of the Institute of Further
Education.

1953

After her coronation the Queen and Prince Philip, Duke of Edinburgh
entered Windsor from Eton High Street in an open carriage.

1954

Mains drainage reached Old Windsor when Taylor Woodrow built an estate
on Cell Farm.

1956

Electric street lights replaced the gas lights at Old Windsor.
Clewer Park, which had been the home of Sir Daniel Gooch, was demolished.

*Clewer Park just before
demolition*

1956
cont.
Dedworth Baptists had to leave the Tin Chapel because the owners wanted to sell the land, which was needed to build a new road. Services were held in a Nissen hut in Abbots Walk and then transferred to Dedworth Green School. Sunday School was held in the Working Men's Club in Dedworth Road, now the site of St Mark's Catholic Church.

1957
15th February Dedworth took on a new status with the creation of the new Conventional District of Dedworth. The Priest Missioner was Rev. Alan R Methuen, previously curate at Clewer responsible for Dedworth.
The owners of Butlers Farm in Dedworth were refused planning permission to build houses due to the lack of services.
£1 Houses! A government scheme allowed the council to offer £1 down houses. Brand new properties in Burnetts Road, Dedworth, were sold for a £1 deposit and the council granted a mortgage of £2,399 or £2,499.

1958
The first owners took possession of their £1 down houses.
Clewer Camera Club was formed by Harry Graves and his wife.
Windsor Boys Club was founded by Ken Burman at Clewer Parish Hall. It lasted for 32 years.
Sites in Dedworth Road were rescheduled as shopping sites including the corner of Greenacre and the corner of Smith's Lane.

The shops at the corner of Smiths Lane in 2000

1959
Rebuilding of Combermere Barracks was begun and continued until 1963. Queen Elizabeth II visited King Edward VII Hospital on the occasion of its Golden Jubilee.
A new Baptist Church was opened in Smith's Lane Dedworth.
Levertons took over the factory on the Rays at Dedworth. The factory was previously the home of R White's Lemonade. Throughout the year 2000 the site was being rebuilt and will be known as Windsor Office Park.

1960   *15th September* **Like a Cathedral Underground!** Official opening of a
        new underground reservoir off Winkfield Road at St Leonard's Hill. The
        reservoir holds three million gallons of water and there is a booster station at
        Eton. There is also a small pump in Wolf Lane.
        The Freedom of the Borough given to the Duke of Edinburgh's Royal Regiment.

1961   The Queen visited Beaumont College at Old Windsor on the occasion of its
        centenary.
        The Crown Estates Act received royal assent. This act states that the
        character of the Windsor Estate owned by the crown must be maintained.
        Old Windsor Memorial Hall was built.

        Workshop for the Elderly Spencer Denney Memorial Workshop was
        initiated by Windsor and Eton Rotary Club providing a meeting place and work
        with a small payment for elderly people. The first workshop was in the
        Congregational Church in William Street. It subsequently moved to Park
        Corner off Clewer Hill Road.
        King's Court School in Old Windsor was opened by Sir John Wolfenden. It
        was on the site of Burford Lodge and served as a primary school for children
        5-11. In 1978 it became a first school for 5-9 year olds.

        Windsor's First Facelift. Street furniture was tidied and the buildings near
        the castle were painted in co-ordinated colours. The curtain wall round the
        castle was removed.

Mr and Mrs Theatre

John Counsell ran the Theatre Royal, Windsor from 1938 until 1987. **Mary Kerridge**, his wife,
and a most distinguished actress, was a never failing support and together they made Windsor's
theatre a place of charm and artistic excellence. Over the years they employed literally thousands
of actors, writers and designers. There has been a theatre in Windsor since Elizabethan times - it
seems, shall we say, to have suited the people of the town. The present theatre was built in 1910
on the site of a previous one that had burned down. It had been turned into a cinema in 1923. And
there, one afternoon, John Counsell, an out-of-work, penniless actor, came to watch a film, and
made a vow to put it back to its proper use. Counsell had had a dream of running his own theatre,
and through various vicissitudes, succeeded in becoming the Licensee (though he never actually
owned the building). During the Second World War the theatre was packed, and a loyal audience
attended every week, a pattern that was to continue for decades. When Counsell's health failed
him, he handed over the Theatre Royal to Mark Piper.

Elizabeth Counsell

1962   Some scenes from the film *On the Beat* starring Norman Wisdom were shot in Windsor. Much of the area used has since been demolished and replaced by Ward Royal, although the film does show some views of Peascod Street. The Ricky Tick Club ran R'n'B nights at the Star and Garter in Peascod Street. Many up and coming rock bands played there including The Rolling Stones. The club later moved to Clewer Mead, though this was advertised as the Thames Hotel.
14th December West Windsor Residents Association was formed.
Butlers Furniture Store at 35 and 37 St Leonard's Road was destroyed by fire (New Year's Eve).

The great freeze of 1963 began in December 1962.

1963   **The Great Freeze**. The River Thames froze over and Bill Wing, of the Bells of Ouseley at Old Windsor, set up tables and served drinks on the ice. Many sports events were cancelled, but 'The Royals' football team played their cup tie against Eastbourne and lost. The people of Windsor suffered power cuts and burst pipes.
The Commons Registration Act under which Doris Mellor later registered Bachelors' Acre as a town green was passed by Parliament.
Baroness Schroder opened an extension to Old Windsor Methodist Church.
Some scenes from the Film *Carry on Cabby* were made in Windsor, starring Sid James and Hattie Jacques.
A new swimming pool was opened at Clewer Mead.

1964   The Household Cavalry Museum was opened by the main gate of the Combermere Barracks.
October New Windsor Community Association formed.

Windsor County Girls' School moved to the present site in Imperial Road.

1965   E & C Duffy took over the bakery at 181 Oxford Road.
May The Freedom of the Borough was given to the Household Cavalry.

1966   The Windsor and Eton Relief Road (A332) was opened. It provided a much-needed river crossing point and was also ready to give direct access to the planned M4.
Middle Thames Water Board was formed and took over the water works.
St Leonard's Estate was bought by circus owner Billy Smart.
St Mark's Road fire station was built.
Thames Valley Police was formed and included the Berkshire Police.

1966
cont. **Windsor Civic Week** took place from 27th March to 2nd April. A week of exhibitions and events was supported by many local firms and organisations. Profits from events, which included a ball at Combermere Barracks, were given to charity. On the Saturday, famous people collecting money in buckets, stopped cars on Castle Hill

The Royal Albert Institute building in Sheet Street was sold.

Death of Sir Sidney Camm, Windsor-born and Windsor-educated designer of the Hawker Hurricane and Hunter aircraft.

The house where Sir Sydney Camm grew up as it is in 2000, empty and boarded up. The blue plaque has been stolen since the photograph was taken.

West Windsor Residents Association put up three candidates for the council and they were all elected.

New Post Office A new post office opened at 38-39 Peascod Street, formerly the site of Creaks outfitters. The post office is still there now with the sorting office behind, entered from William Street.

The 6th National Jazz and Blues Festival was held at Royal Windsor Racecourse at the end of July.

1967 Dedworth Baptist Church became independent from Windsor Baptists.

Beaumont College at Old Windsor closed.

The maternity ward at Old Windsor Hospital was closed and services were transferred to Upton Hospital at Slough.

The 7th National Jazz and Blues Festival was held at Balloon Meadow in early August.

1968   The Freedom of the Borough was given to the Brigade of Guards.
        St Mark's Catholic Church at Dedworth was built.

*When the Catholic
Church at Dedworth was
new in 1968*

1969   Windsor Festival Society was founded.
        4th July In a ceremony at the Guildhall, Windsor was officially twinned with
        Goslar. The twinning document was signed by Wilhelm Degenhardt, mayor of
        Goslar and Ian Keeler, mayor of Windsor. Since that time many Windsor
        residents have visited Goslar and have hosted visitors from the German town.
        22nd July Safari Park was opened in the grounds of St Leonard's.
        Inaugural concert of the Compton Theatre Organ in Old Windsor Memorial Hall.
        The Guildhall was redecorated.
        Ward Royal was completed and awarded a medal and a diploma for good
        design, despite the fact that the local people disliked it. A story went around
        the town at the time that a stunned American tourist asked why the local
        prison was so close to the town centre.

1970   Windsor Bridge was declared unsafe and closed to traffic. It was later paved
        over and seats provided for tourists. In the year 2000 it became even more
        unsafe and measures were taken to prevent too many people congregating on it.
        All Saints Church Dedworth was demolished because of land slippage and the
        effect of the bomb in 1944.
        Some restoration was work done on the Guildhall. The necessity for this was
        discovered during the previous year's redecoration.
        The first Windsor International Driving Grand Prix took place. Stage coaches
        drawn by eight horses were seen in parts of the town.
        The children's wards at Old Windsor Hospital were closed.
        Scenes from the film *Carry on Loving* were made in Windsor.

1971   The M4 was opened to traffic. Direct access for Windsor drivers was
        available from the Windsor and Eton Relief Road.
        The last Court of Quarter Sessions was held in the Guildhall.
        The premises of New Windsor Community Association were opened by
        Queen Elizabeth the Queen Mother.

1972   *20th May* Old Windsor Methodist Church was rededicated after the building had
        been refurbished and the altar table relocated at the opposite end of the building.
        First Windsor Free Festival. Several thousand young people set up camp in
        Windsor Great Park and vowed never to pay rent again. They were
        unorganised and anarchistic. Their music disturbed local residents and they
        destroyed property. Illegal drugs were circulated.
        The film *No Sex Please, We're British,* was made in Windsor. The story,
        which concerns a Windsor Bank, featured Barclays Bank on the corner of the
        High Street and Peascod Street.
        Windsor and Maidenhead Symphony Orchestra was founded.
        The foundation stone of Dedworth's new All Saints Church was laid by Rt
        Revd Eric Wild, Bishop of Reading.

1973   **Second Windsor Free Festival** was held. Once again local people were
        upset by the antics of the visitors.
        7th June Elections for the Windsor and Maidenhead District Council were held. The
        new council was granted permission to use the word Royal in its new name.
        Thames Side House, which was built on the site of a farm on the river bank
        under the castle, was opened as Barclays Bank's local head office. This was
        transferred from the premises on the corner of Peascod Street and High
        Street which had been shared with the local branch since 1917.
        Work began on the Queen Anne Court development in Lower Peascod Street.
        John Procter was the last Mayor of Windsor, an office that dated from 1363.
        The new All Saints, Church at Dedworth was consecrated.

1974 *1st April* **The New Borough** The Royal Borough of New Windsor combined with Maidenhead Borough, Windsor Rural District, Maidenhead Rural District, Eton Urban District and part of Eton Rural District to form the Royal Borough of Windsor and Maidenhead, which took over from the Windsor and Maidenhead District Council. The first mayor of the new borough was Kit Aston.

Third Windsor Free Festival. The festival got so out of hand that it was terminated by the police after six days. Some of the hippies who took part set a tree alight and then prevented a fire engine from attending. After the festival the Windsor Citizens Action Group was set up to prevent the people of Windsor ever having to endure the nightmare of a free festival again.

The Battler for Bachelors' Acre

Doris Mellor was born in St Mark's Road Windsor and studied history at London University. She then spent 30 years teaching in South Africa. After retirement she returned to St Mark's Road and in the 1960s she could be seen around Windsor investigating requests for planning permission to ensure that none of the historic buildings were unnecessarily altered or destroyed. Often wearing a tweed suit and always in a hat, she would fearlessly confront owners and architects. In 1966 she became the first secretary of the Landscape sub-committee of the Windsor and Eton Society. The Society and many other local people were horrified when the council proposed to build a multi-storey car park on Bachelors' Acre. Doris diligently researched the history of the Acre and found that this was not the first time it had been threatened. She began a battle to preserve it as a green lung close to the centre of Windsor. With the full support of the Windsor and Eton Society she registered the Acre as a Town Green. The registration was opposed by the council. The fight went from court to court, sometimes the council won, sometimes it was Doris. Finally on 20th May 1975 at the highest court in the land, the House of Lords, Doris was supported by Lord Denning who decided that Bachelors' Acre was subject to a customary right of the inhabitants to indulge in lawful sports and pastimes. Doris was a national heroine when the story appeared in the press, and she was awarded an MBE in 1977.

Pamela Marson

1975   Charles, Prince of Wales, became High Steward of the Royal Borough of Windsor and Maidenhead.

Wellmans ironmonger's shop in Peascod Street was pulled down.

Queen Anne Court development in Lower Peascod Street was completed.

Windsor Community Arts Centre founded.

Windsor Morris, an all-female team of Morris dancers was formed and they held their first public dance in May.

East Berkshire College was renamed Windsor and Maidenhead College when the new Langley building of Slough College became the most eastern College of Further Education in the county.

1976   Windsor Local History Publications Group was formed to ensure that the history of the town was researched and recorded.

A Fighter for History

'It was his love of Windsor's past that spurred him to defend it against what he believed to be ham-fisted or insensitive incursions by modern developers.' *Windsor Observer*, 12th November 1999. This sentence from **Gordon Cullingham**'s obituary seems to sum up the life he led after his retirement from the position of Borough Engineer of Windsor in 1974.

Born in Beckenham, Kent, in 1915, Gordon came to Windsor in 1939 to work in the engineers department of New Windsor Borough Council. Eventually he was appointed Borough Engineer. This work brought him into contact with the public buildings that he grew to love. He was a relentless researcher and note taker, and could be relied on to make every effort to answer any question put to him on the history of the town. He brought the work of several great Windsorians to the attention of the public, writing books on Old Windsor Tapestries and Stained Glass factories, PY Alexander, the aviator, and FJ Camm, the brother of Sir Sidney.

He was elected Chairman of Windsor Local History Publications Group in 1981 and when he retired following a heart attack in 1988 he was made first Life President.

His last research work is in this book as he had completed his first allotted task, to find the dates of public services such as gas, electricity and water, shortly before his death.

Pamela Marson

1977   The 700th anniversary of Windsor's first Charter coincided with the Queen's Silver Jubilee year. As part of the celebrations the Queen lit a beacon on Snow Hill and this was a signal to light a chain of bonfires across the country. There was also a pageant of the history of Windsor involving children from all the schools in the town on Bachelors' Acre.

The former Royal Albert Institution building was rebuilt as offices.

Doris Mellor was awarded an MBE.

1978   Windsor County Boys School and Windsor County Girls School changed their names to Windsor Boys School and Windsor Girls School when they became comprehensive. The Royal Free School and Princess Margaret Rose School joined to become Princess Margaret Royal Free School. They all became 13-18 upper schools. Other schools became first or middle schools.

       Revd Ivy Halden was appointed minister of the United Reformed Church, as the Congregational Church of England and Wales became after it united with the Presbyterian Church of England in 1972. She was the first woman to hold such a position in any Windsor Church.

1979   King Edward Court was built.

       Part of Windsor Central Station was acquired by Madame Tussauds to build a tourist attraction initially named Royalty and Railways.

       4th November The foundation stone of Christchurch United Reformed Church in William Street was laid on the site of the recently demolished Congregational Church.

'Sunny' South

Raymond South came to Windsor in 1930 to teach history at Windsor County Boys School having obtained his degree at Oxford. He spent 38 years at the school and was deputy head when he retired. He joined the Labour party in Windsor, was the constituency secretary, and was elected to the council in 1945. He retired from council work in 1974 when the borough merged with Maidenhead. He was a founder member and chairman of the Windsor and Eton Society. Raymond and his wife Marjorie, who was also a teacher and a county councillor, both spent a life time of service to others. Raymond inspired two generations of Windsor boys to love history and also natural history. His particular interest was ornithology. After his retirement much of his time was devoted to local history and he was most generous with the help he gave to others. With a professional attitude and gentle manner he ensured that members of Windsor Local History Publications Group were well aware of good research methods and the dangers of misinterpretation. He wrote many books and articles about Windsor including *The Book of Windsor* in 1977 to coincide with the septcentenary celebrations. He died in Windsor at the age of 92 in December 1999 and a quiet Quaker funeral was held. A memorial service at Windsor Methodist Church was attended by boys he inspired forty to sixty years earlier, the boys who named him 'Sunny' South.

Pamela Marson

1980   Major reorganisation of education in Windsor completed.

       York House was built in Sheet Street, bringing some of the administration back to the town.

       12th October The new United Reformed Church was opened.

1981   Clewer Local History Museum was founded in the Church Lodge at St
        Andrew's Church, Mill Lane, by Rev. Denis Shaw, Rector of Clewer.
        The Kipling Building, which had been the centre of Windsor's administration
        was demolished.
        Windsor Community Arts Centre moved into the Old Court and Fire Station.

1982   King Edward Horse Hall was demolished.
        President Reagan arrived for a state visit by helicopter.
        Rank-Hovis built a new headquarters on the site of the Kipling building.
        The Guildhall Exhibition closed and the artefacts were returned to the small
        Museum Store at Tinkers' Lane in Dedworth.
        1st May Dedworth became a Parish in its own right and minor alterations
        were made to the areas of other Parishes. The first Vicar was Rev. John
        Stone, who had been Priest Missioner for six years.
        Rotary Club of Windsor St George was founded.

1983   *Easter* Madame Tussauds Royalty and Railways Exhibition opened in
        Windsor Central Station. It included an exhibition of *Victorian Life in
        Windsor*, organised by the Royal Borough Museum Collection. Some of the
        visitors expected a huge railway centre and the name was changed to Royalty
        and Empire shortly afterwards.
        The cinema close to Windsor Bridge closed after 54 years. It had recently
        been renamed the Carousel by Lord (Billy) Smart, but was known previously
        as the Playhouse, an ABC cinema.
        Maxwell's grocery closed after 80 years in Alexandra Road.
        A medieval hearth was discovered in Knights Close, Dedworth, and was
        dated to approximately 1350.
        Windsor's archives were transferred to Berkshire Record Office.
        The George V Memorial was refurbished and re-opened by the Queen Mother.

1984   The rear part of Windsor Baptist Church was demolished when part of the
        roof fell in.
        The bus garage opposite the King Edward VII Hospital, operated by London
        Passenger Transport Board, was closed and replaced by a bus station in
        Slough.

1986   Complete rebuilding of Victoria Barracks was undertaken at a cost of £50m.
        (to 1993).
        Dyson's jewellery business closed after 101 years in Windsor's Thames Street.
        Three members of West Windsor Residents Association were elected to the
        Windsor and Maidenhead Council.

1987   Moore's Imperial Bus Service closed. Many Dedworth residents mourned the loss of a truly friendly service.
Jennings yard, next to the river, was excavated by Wessex Archaeology and evidence of medieval buildings found.
The first Summer Exhibition by the Royal Borough Collection was held at the Guildhall. It was on Medieval Windsor.

1988   *October* Opening ceremony of the pedestrianised Lower Peascod Street.

1991   Old Windsor Hospital finally closed.
Edgington, Spink and Hyne, architects who had been in Windsor for 135 years, moved to new offices in Datchet.
Work began on the restoration of Windsor Methodist Church in Alma Road. During the work services were held at St Edward's Church's Parish Centre.

Windsor Methodist Church in 1991

Madame Tussauds sold the lease of the site of the Royalty and Empire Exhibition at Windsor Central Station to L & R Leisure as a going concern. The *Victorian Life in Windsor* Exhibition contained within it was dismantled. However, it was not long before the whole exhibition was closed and that part of the station was re-built as a shopping complex.

1992   *September* The Methodist Chapel on the corner of Alma Road was re-opened after virtually being rebuilt, retaining only the outer walls. The sanctury is now at the level of the old gallery and a lift has been installed. The ground floor has meeting rooms, offices, a modern kitchen and toilets.

1992   **Fire at the Castle** The eyes of the world were on Windsor while our castle
cont.   burned. The centre of the town was closed and local people and firms helped
fire services from the whole region. The fire was found to have been caused
by an electric light setting fire to a curtain in a private chapel during a major
period of refurbishment.

Duffys Bakery, 181 Oxford Road closed. This bakery, previously known as E
Hicks & Son, had served the public for 111 years.

1993   *6th April* The Queen and the Duke of Edinburgh were present at the re-
dedication of Windsor Methodist Church.
2nd September The Scots Guards moved into their newly re-built Victoria
Barracks.
Windsor and Maidenhead College merged with Langley College and the name
reverted to East Berkshire College.
Tesco opened a supermarket in Dedworth. The new store had a major effect
on the lives of the people in west Windsor. Two previous supermarkets had
been established in the middle of Windsor town. Waitrose is still in King
Edward Court but International Stores, which was in William Street changed
hands several times and then closed

A Noble River

The ancient highway of the **River Thames** has always been important for Windsor. The castle
was built on a chalk bluff above the Thames making it easier to defend, and to do this most of the
wood, stone and provisions were brought by river to the little port below. There were three
breweries in the town at one time and beer was sent away by river to other places. Access to the
town by road meant that a bridge had to be built and the old wooden bridges were constantly
being repaired, resulting in tolls and pontage being charged for traffic moving over and under.
These tolls were finally abolished on 1st December 1898. An iron bridge was erected by Charles
Hollis between 1821 and 1824 and Thomas Telford was the Consulting Engineer. This was deemed
unsafe and closed to vehicular traffic in 1970 as a new road bridge, named the Elizabeth Bridge,
had been built further upstream in 1966. There is also a railway bridge built in 1849 by Brunel. An
annual traditional feature on the river is the swan upping when the Dyers and Vintners Companies
and the keeper of the Queen's swans check the birds and mark the cygnets.

Instead of a boggy and smelly meadow on the banks of the river a fine promenade has
been made and Alexandra Gardens provide a relaxing area. Everyone can enjoy the River Thames
at Windsor today and the boats only take passengers on trips up and down stream for pleasure.
In the past swimmers had to use the river and army horses were taken into the water too. Now
there is a fine Leisure Pool complex and open space for residents and visitors to relax and picnic.

Beryl Hedges

The Royal Borough Museum Collection

In 1866 Queen Victoria offered 'a Roman tomb, a cinerary urn, several British bronze Celts, portions of an ancient canoe, stags horns of very great antiquity and Elizabethan tobacco pipes' to 'the Museum about to be formed'. This museum closed in 1921.

The idea resurfaced in 1949 with a successful exhibition at the Guildhall by the Windsor and Eton Society. But the actual beginning of what was to become the Royal Borough Museum Collection coincided with the Festival of Britain and the restoration of the Guildhall in 1951. A modest selection of the wealth of material donated by local people was displayed in the downstairs room and known as the Guildhall Exhibition. When it closed in 1982 the honorary curator, Judith Hunter, and a small group of volunteers transferred everything to a very small room in Royal Borough of Windsor and Maidenhead's Operations Unit at Tinker's Lane. Pressure was relieved briefly when some Victorian artefacts were loaned to the Royalty and Empire Exhibition at the Western Region Station in 1983, but these were returned when the exhibition closed in the 1990s.

Gradually the space doubled - and then doubled again - to form two long rooms, one stuffed to the ceiling with artefacts, paintings, prints, maps and books, and the other used as an office, library, storage area for photographs and old exhibition boards, workroom and study area for visitors using the Collection as a resource centre.

Geological and archaeological items include a fossilised sea urchin found by a school boy in a Dedworth garden. A number of objects are unique to Windsor - the 1911 aerial post box and the engine of the first petrol-driven aeroplane designed by Sydney Camm, although this is on loan to Brooklands Museum at the moment.

Judith (now Dr Judith) retired in 2000 and we begin a new century with a new, full-time curator, Olivia Gooden. Perhaps we could celebrate with a new Museum, just 134 years after it was first suggested?

Damaris Graham

Tesco Store at Dedworth in 2000

1994   The old Royal Free Middle School building on Bachelors' Acre was refurbished and turned into flats.
        12th April The Duke of Edinburgh opened the pedestrianised Peascod Street.

1995   *Town and Crown,* an exhibition of Windsor's heritage, opened above the Information Centre at 24 High Street Windsor and a new Public Library opened next to Bachelors' Acre.
        Daniel's Department Store was completely refurbished.
        11th May VE Day commemoration celebrations.
        Noah's Ark public house closed.

1996   Prince Philip, Duke of Edinburgh, was granted the Freedom of the Borough in a ceremony at the Guildhall.
        March Wellesley House, Vansittart Road, a hostel for young offenders closed.
        The Danish firm of Lego bought St Leonard's, formerly Safari Park, and opened Legoland Windsor.
        A major flood relief scheme for the whole of the Royal Borough began. Channels are being built north of the borough to divert surplus water. This has involved temporary re-routing of the M4 motorway, and the freezing of the ground beneath a bridge at Taplow. The scheme will not be completed for several years, when landscaping will provide natural habitats for wild life.

Working for Wildlife

In 1987 following a meeting at Windsor and Maidenhead College, an urban wildlife group was formed under the auspices of the Berks, Bucks and Oxon Naturalists Trust (now the BBO Wildlife Trust). The main purpose of the group was to enhance the wildlife potential of local sites. The first task was litter-picking in Roses Lane, Dedworth. Local people were recruited to help with work at Hemwood Dell and Castle Farm Spinney at Dedworth, as well as sites in Maidenhead where they have planted trees and cleared storm damage. The group cut the grass at Sutherland Grange and helped to conserve the wildlife in the Bourne Ditch when houses were built on the site in Osborne Road. The group is currently working at the Clewer pond and intends to survey the new flood relief channel to ensure that the wildlife is preserved.

Colin Gray

1997   The state apartments at the castle were reopened to the public after spectacular restoration, involving craftsmanship of the highest order.

1998   *1st April* The Royal Borough of Windsor and Maidenhead became a unitary authority after Berkshire County Council was abolished. Among other things, the town became responsible for education and libraries.

1998
cont. There was an abortive attempt by the council to change Windsor's education system again. There was massive public opposition to a return to infant, junior and secondary schools in favour of the current first, middle and upper schools.

1999 *29th March* Windsor Magistrates' Court closed after 560 years of justice being dispensed locally. The new East Berkshire bench sits at Slough, Bracknell and Maidenhead.
10th April Thames Valley Athletics Centre, the new home of the Windsor, Slough and Eton Athletics Club was opened at Pococks Lane Eton.
27th May Fire swept through Combermere Barracks destroying the possessions of members of the Household Cavalry who were serving in Macedonia.
19th June Prince Edward, Earl of Wessex, and his bride Sophie Rhys-Jones, drove round the streets of Windsor after their marriage at St George's Chapel.
23rd December Royal Windsor Racecourse was sold by David Thompson of Hillsdown Holdings to Arena Leisure for £13.6m. Racing is to continue.

2000 All Saints Church Dedworth was enlarged and extensively refurbished - services were temporarily held at St Mark's Catholic Church.
Dedworth Baptist Church was gutted by fire. Services were held at Dedworth School, including the 40th anniversary celebration.
20th May Old Windsor Methodist Church was re-dedicated after it was refurbished and a tower feature added exactly 28 years after the previous refurbishment.

Old Windsor Methodist Church after refurbishment

Windsor Central Station now includes a shopping precinct

The Royal Waiting Room is now a Bar and Canteen

Queen Charlotte Street is the shortest street in England

Windsor Dials is the Towns newest Development

2000 The Royal Borough of Windsor and Maidenhead produced their own web site.
cont.

Old Windsor Working Men's Club admitted women for the first time and changed its name to the Old Windsor Club.

Princess Margaret Royal Free School closed.

The sisters of the Community of St John the Baptist in Hatch Lane prepared to leave the area after 148 years.

Two of the nuns who are leaving Windsor checking their own web site

EPILOGUE

A thousand years ago the people who lived in the Windsor
area would have been part of a small family group.
People who lived a few miles away
would have been thought of as foreigners
and the invaders such as the Danes, and earlier the Romans,
came from places that were quite unimaginable.

In the year 2000 Windsorians regard those from other towns
only as rivals in a sporting contest.
Foreigners come from other continents
and there is an unimaginable universe out there.

What will the next thousand years bring?
Will the world be our family and foreigners be from other galaxies?
And what will be unimaginable then?

Appendix

Listings of Mayors of New Windsor
This list is taken from the board in the Guildhall at Windsor.
Since it was first painted Mrs Shelagh Bond has found evidence that
John Payntour was called Mayor of Windsor in 1363, which is
earlier than the first date given on the board.

Mayors of The Royal Borough of Windsor and Maidenhead
Chairmen of Old Windsor Parish Council

Vicars of Windsor
Windsor Team Ministry
Vicars of Old Windsor
Rectors of Clewer
Curates and Vicars of All Saints Dedworth
Priests in charge of St Agnes, Spital
Parish Priests of St Edwards Roman Catholic Church
Priests in Charge at St Mark's Dedworth
Ministers of Windsor Congregational Church
(now United Reformed Church)
Ministers of Windsor Baptist Church
Ministers of Dedworth Baptist Church
Ministers of Windsor Methodist Church

**Mayors of New Windsor
as listed in the Guildhall**

Richard II

1382	John Lausell
1389	Robert Honeswurth
1392	John Lausell
1394	John Gardiner
1395	John Lausell

Henry IV

1403	Thomas Harpecote
1404	Robert Wythele
1407	Richard Merkham

Henry V

1413	Robert Wythele

Henry VI

1423	Ralph Cheppys
1427	Nicholas Larewood
1438	Ralph Cheppys
1441	William Towe
1443	John Avelyn
1448	William Towe MP
1449	John Avelyn
1450	John Ottewey
1453	Hugh Aylewyn
1454	William Towe
1455	Hugh Aylewyn
	William Towe
1456	William Towe
1457	John Avelyn
1459	Roger Wayte

Edward IV

1461	John Goodman
1464	John Avelyn

1465	Edmund Pury
1467	John Goodman
1469	William Bullok
1471	Edmund Pury
1473	Edmund Pury
	William Bullok
1474	Edmund Pury
1476	William Hether
1477	Edmund Pury
1478	William Hether

Edward V Richard III

1483	Thomas Engely

Henry VII

1487	John Todde
1489	William Canon
1490	Nicholas Larewood
1491	John Todde
1492	John Baker
1494	John Todde
1495	Thomas Whiteley
1500	Thomas Todde
1501	Thomas Ryder
1502	John Scott
1503	Thomas Buckenell
1504	John Cony
1505	William Cannon
1507	Robert Staple
1508	John Hether

Henry VIII

1510	Andrew Bereman
1512	Thomas Rider
1513	John Scott
1514	Hugh Starkey
1515	John Todd
1516	John Hether
1517	Thomas Benet

1518 Andrew Bereman
1519 William Pury
1520 John Bykforde
1521 Thomas Benet
1522 Christoper Staper
1523 William Pury
1524 Geoffrey More
1525 Andrew Bereman
1526 Thomas Benet
1527 John Fenn
1529 William Symonds
1531 Richard Puvis
1532 James Cales
1533 William Thorpe
1534 James Prince
1535 William Snowball
1536 Robert Benet
1537 Richard Puvis
1538 John Rollys
1539 Matthew Gwynne
1540 Richard Fitzwater
1541 Henry Holden
1542 WilliamSymons
1543 William Snowball
1544 John Pury
1545 Matthew Gwynne
1546 Thomas Ryder

Edward VI

1547 Richard Fawcon
1548 Matthew Gwynne
1549 Thomas Goode
1550 Robert Sadock
1551 John Tyle
1552 Thomas Goode

Mary I

1553 Richard Archer
1554 Andrew Alley
1555 John Westcott

1556 Thomas Butler
1557 Andrew Alley

Elizabeth I

1558 Gabriel Hylle
1559 William Hanley
1560 John Whiteley
1561 Richard Gallys MP
1562 Thomas Ryder
1563 William Lawrence
1564 Richard Temple
1566 Richard Gallys
1567 Thomas Goade
1568 John Whiteley
1570 Richard Gallys
1573 Richard Redford
1575 William Jacob
1578 Richard Temple
1580 Thomas Aston
1581 Richard Temple
1582 Richard Needham
1583 Richard Redford
      Richard Needham
1584 Thomas Clifton
1585 Edward Hake
1586 Robert Bradshaw
1587 William Gwynne
1588 Henry Harris
1592 Thomas Alden
1594 John Frymley
1596 Richard Washington
1597 Thomas Alden
1598 Christopher Davies
1599 Thomas Hayse
1600 Richard Washington
1601 Robert Cawcott
1602 Humphrey Fawcett

James I

1603 Henry Harris

1604   Sylvester Sweetzer
1605   Thomas Alden
1606   Richard Washington
1607   Humphrey Fawcett
1608   Richard Masleyn
1609   Robert Lowe
1610   Matthew Daye
1611   Richard Wympe
1612   Sylvester Sweetzer
1613   Richard Washington
1614   Christopher Davys
1615   Humphrey Fawcett
1616   Sylvester Sweetzer
1617   Robert Lowe
1618   Matthew Daye
1620   William Fisher
1621   Matthew Daye
1622   Richard Wympe
1623   John Wickes

Charles I

1625   Francis Jones
1626   George Starkey
1627   Charles Burges
1628   Richard Loke
1629   Robert Lowe
1630   Matthew Daye
1631   Richard Wympe
1632   John Wickes
1633   Hercules Trew
1634   Francis Jones
1635   George Starkey
1636   Thomas Havergill
1637   Charles Burges
1638   Richard Noke
1639   Richard Nash
1640   Henry Hall
1641   Anthony Watts
1642   William Church
       Matthew Daye
1643   Hercules Trew

1644   John Wickes
1645   George Starkey
1646   Charles Burges
1647   Richard Church
1648   Thomas Chapman

Commonwealth

1649   Silvester Sweetzer
1650   William Mills
1651   Samuel Mihill
1652   William Stevenson
1653   Henry Fooks
1654   John Hatch
1655   Richard Nash
1656   William Poole
1657   Ralph Brown
1658   Matthew Saye
1659   William Galland

Charles II

1660   Richard Noke
       Richard Church
1661   Samuel Mihill
1662   Richard Nash
1663   William Poole
1664   William Galland
1665   Henry Choone
1666   George Saye
1667   John Randall
1668   William Rowe
1669   Thomas Merwin
1670   John Church
1671   John Nash
1672   Thomas Addams
1673   George Saye
1674   Francis Hill
1675   William Carey
1676   Thomas White
1677   Robert Frith
1678   Roger Olive

1679 John Randall
1680 William Row
1681 Thomas Merwin
1682 John Church
1683 Thomas Adams
1684 Francis Hill

James II

1685 William Chiffinch
1686 James Graham
1687 James Bridgeman
1688 Charles Potts
       Robert Frith

William III Mary II

1689 Thomas Ducke
1690 Moses Bruche
1691 Silas Seabrowe
1692 Nathaniel Lyford
1693 Henry Ason
1694 John Porter
1695 Thomas Rutter
1696 Giles Aldridge
1697 Samuel Gilman
1698 Samuel Chapman
1699 Giles Saunders
1700 Thomas Ducke
1701 Nathaniel Lyford
       Henry Ason
       Thomas Ducke

Anne

1702 John Porter
1703 Thomas Rutter
1704 Giles Aldridge
1705 Samuel Gilman
1706 Samuel Chapman
1707 Giles Saunders
1708 John Clark

1709 Thomas Winwood
1710 John Pemberton
1711 Jeremiah Bennett
1712 Nathaniel Hamond
1713 Thomas Shefford

George 1

1714 William Davis
1715 William Sumner
1716 Richard Reeve
1717 Thomas Rutter
1718 Samuel Gilman
1719 John Pemberton
1720 Thomas Shefford
1721 William Sumner
1722 Richard Reeve
1723 Richard Hill
1724 Henry Ason
1725 Thomas Rutter
       Samuel Gilman
1726 John Pemberton

George II

1727 Thomas Shefford
1728 Richard Reeve
1729 Richard Hill
1730 Henry Ason
1731 Theophilis Hobbs
1732 Thomas Bryer
1733 Benjamin Palmer
1734 James Poole
1735 John Snowden
1736 Thomas Rowland
1737 Thomas Rutter
1738 Anthy Bedingfield
1739 Richard Hope
       John Shefford
       Lord Sidney Beauclerk
1740 Lord Sidney Beauclerk
       Henry Reddington

1741 Francis Cooper
1742 William Hatch
1743 Robert Dary
1744 William May
1745 John Herring
1746 Thomas Rutter
1747 John Snowden
1748 Anthy Bedingfield
1749 William Hatch
1750 Robert Dary
      John Herring
1751 Henry Coombs
1752 Lord George Beauclerk
      William May
1753 John Snowden
1754 William Brereton
1755 John Williams
1756 Robert Edwards
1757 John Snowden
1758 Thomas Rutter
1759 George Hatch

George III

1760 Henry Foster
1761 Henry Coombs
1762 Richard Pinnock
1763 Richard Bradbury
1764 John Carr
1765 John Benning
1766 William Tyrrell
1767 Richard Pinnock
1768 Richard Seaward
1769 Benjamin Burt
1770 Joseph Snow
1771 William Kimberly
1772 George Hatch
1773 Henry Coombs
1774 John Carr
1775 John Benning
1776 William Tyrrell
1777 Richard Seaward

1778 Thomas Barrow
1779 Thomas Loathis
1780 Joseph Snow
1781 Joseph Bending
1782 William Kimberly
1783 James Panton
1784 George Hatch
1785 Joseph Bending
1786 Joseph Snow
1787 Giles Webb
1788 James Panton
1789 Joseph Snow
1790 John Banyard
1791 James Webb
1792 John Slingsby
1793 Paul Perryman
1794 Richd. Remington
      Joseph Bending
1795 Robert Blunt
1796 John Snow
1797 James Eglestone
1798 John Slingsby
1799 Edward Parker
1800 John Snowden
1801 Paul Perryman
      John Slingsby
1802 William Hanson
1803 James Atkins
1804 Charles Grantham
1805 William Thomas
1806 Charles Knight
1807 James Eglestone
1808 James Coombs
1809 Edward Bovingdon
1810 James Millns
1811 Edward Parker
1812 John Snowden
1813 WilliamHanson
1814 John Hatch
1815 James Atkins
1816 Charles Layton
1817 Charles Knight

1818   Edward Bovingdon
1819   George Davis

George IV

1820   John Banister
1821   James Egleston
1822   John Chapman
1823   Charles Layton
1824   Edward Brown
1825   John Clode
1826   John Voules
1827   Thomas Jenner
1828   Robert Tebbot
1829   James Church

William IV

1830   John Banister
1831   John Clode
1832   Charles Snowden
1833   Robert Blunt
1834   William Legh
1836   Edward Bovingdon

Victoria

1837   William Benning
1838   Charles Snowden
1839   William Berridge
1840   John Banister
1841   John Clode
1842   Robert Tebbot
1843   Robert Blunt
1844   Thomas Clarke
1845   Thomas Adams
1846   James Bedborough
1847   William Berridge
1848   Frederick Twinch
1849   William Hanson
1850   Charles Phillips
1851   Charles Layton

1852   W B Holderness
1853   Henry Darvill
       James Bedborough
1854   John Clode
1855   James Brown
1856   Geoffrey Pearl
1857   W Seaward-Cantrell
1858   John Jones
1859   Thomas Nixon
1860   Henry Driver
1861   W B Holderness
1862   William Hanson
1863   Thomas Cleave
1864   W Redford Harris
1865   John Jones
1866   F K Copeland
1867   John Wm Wellman
1868   Thos Chamberlain
1869   Joseph Devereux
1870   William Mason
1871   Hy William Jones
1872   W Seaward Cantrell
1873   John Jones
1874   William Underhay
1875   James Brown
1876   James Dewe
1878   John Wm Wellman
1879   John Webb
1880   George Tuck
1881   Joseph Devereux
1882   Sir Joseph Devereux
1883   J Oberlin Harris
1885   Joseph Lundy
1886   Sir Hy L Simpson
1887   Geo H Peters
1889   John L Hollis
1890   Thomas Dyson
1891   James Brown
1892   Joseph Gane
1893   Fredk A Layton
1894   Henry Webber
1895   Bernard Westlake

1896 Sir George Long
1897 Thomas Clarke
1898 Sir John Soundy
1899 Alf G T Barber
1900 Walter P Reavell

Edward VII

1901 George Mitchell
1902 Alex Wm Shipley
1904 Sir Wm Shipley
1905 John L Hollis
1906 James Brown
1907 Edward Bamfylde
1908 William Carter
1909 C Fredk Dyson

George V

1910 Sir Fredk Dyson
1911 Augustus Harris
1912 Thos Edmund Luff
1913 William Carter
1919 William Fairbank
1920 Robt Geo Rawkins
1921 Sir William Carter
1922 Sir Fredk Dyson
1923 Sir William Carter
1928 Stephen Wright
1930 Rev Harold S Fox
1931 Frank L Ellen
1932 Robt Geo Rawkins
1933 George E Short
1935 Arthur E Churcher

Edward VIII

1936 Sir Arthur Churcher

George VI

1937 Mrs F M Carteret-Carey

1939 Norman C Butler
1943 Alfred W Bull
1946 Frederick I Fuzzens
1949 Richard H Tozer

Elizabeth II

1952 Cyril D Dyson
1953 Sir Cyril D Dyson
1954 Miss G F Hanbury-Williams
1956 Herbert A Barney
1958 John Procter
1960 J Stanley Davis
1961 Francis Burton
1962 Harold H Basford
1963 Mrs M M Pressey
1964 John T Goss
1965 William M Pratt
1966 Ronald F Dyason
1967 John C Deacon
1968 Cyril Herd
1969 John D Keeler
1970 Richard Piner
1971 Francis Burton
       Richard E Shaw
1972 Richard E Shaw
1973 John Proctor

Mayors of the
Royal Borough of
Windsor and Maidenhead

1974 Christopher S Aston
1976 Iain G N Harris
1978 Neville Whiteley
1979 Mrs Joyce K Fotherby
1980 Ronald F Dyason
1981 Arthur L Jacob
1982 Albert J Bellworthy
1983 Mrs Brigide Helbronner
1984 Frank A Robinson
1985 Richard E Shaw

1986 Mrs Shreela Flather	1680 Thomas Doughty
1987 William W Cooley	1702 Thomas Horne
1988 Roy Bennett	1720 Henry Justell
1989 Anthony W. Griffiths	1729 William Burchett
1990 Robin Austin	1750 John Bostock
1991 Miss Ursula E M Badger	1786 William Roberts
1992 Anthony J Langdown	1792 William Foster
1993 Michael A Scott	1827 William H Roberts
1994 Dennis F Outwin	1844 Thomas Thellusson Carter
1995 Bryan L Hedley	1880 Roland Errington
1996 Mrs Adrienne P Sheldon	1900 Arthur T C Cowie
1997 Eric E Wiles	1925 William Elwell
1998 Mrs Kathryn D Newbound	1932 Gerald G Payne- Cook
1999 Mrs Sandra Hopkins	1943 Cyprian Dymoke-Marr
2000 John T H Webb	1971 Denis Shaw

Rectors of Clewer	**Vicars of New Windsor**
1347 Roger Ciffrewast	1219 Alan
1348 Robert de Shareshulle	1228 John
c1363 John de Shareshulle	1321 John d Cateloigne
c1407 John Pesemer	1324 Richard de Midhurst
1417 William Lochard	1335 James de la Croye
Radulph Thomas	1349 Hugh Knight de Estpirie
1431 John Coryngham	1352 John de Wengrave
1444 John Batt	1353 John de Valle
1449 William Cooke	1354 William Mere de Pottern
1450 John Howden	1361 Hugh de Marleburgh
1464 William Harmer	1362 William de Querendon
Nicholas Waldegrave	Thomas de Aston
1479 William Bromwiche	1376 William Walton
1509 William Askynson	1380 John Rode
1511 James Christopherson	1380 Richard Hide
1533 William Knotte	1383 John Clerk
1542 George Parker	1398 William Asswell
1554 Richard Arche	1402 Roger Gerneys
1575 William Smith	1405 William Park
1599 Valentine Carey	1415 Richard Hywet
1603 Hugh Jones	Thomas Fryday
1625 James Jones	1432 Roger Lutterworth
1661 Jerameele Terrent	1436 Robert Waller
1677 Lionel Gatford	1466 Richard Peynter

159

1468	John Chadleworth
1469	Thomas Hether
1485	Thomas Bowden
	George Gard
1488	William Thurlow
1502	William Ingelarde
1516	Geoffrey Wrey
1517	George Wilsett
1547	Stephen Knight
1554	Otevellus Gyles
1583	William Harris
1592	William Butterton
1605	John Moorecroft
1610	John Martyn
1633	John Cleaver
1662	John Heaver
1670	Alexander Read
1680	John Barrow
1685	Samuel Haines
1689	Thomas Merry
1703	Thomas Dawson
1741	John Bostock the Elder
1774	John Bostock the Younger
1798	William Majendie
1800	Joseph Lowthian
1804	Henry Plimley
1817	John Graham
1821	Isaac Gosset
1855	Henry John Ellison
1876	James St John Blunt
1878	Richard Gee
1895	John Henry Joshua Ellison
1913	Ernest Morell Blackie
1921	Clarence Haslewood Hamilton
1940	Ralph Creed Meredith
1958	Leslie Stephen Ronald Badham

Rector of New Windsor

1973 David Nigel Griffiths
St John's Church became part of New
    Windsor Team Ministry in 1981

New Windsor Team Ministry from 1981

Team Rectors

1981	David Nigel Griffiths
1988	Canon Jeffery WalterGeorge Whale

Team Vicars

1989	Jonathan Graham Cruickshank
	(Holy Trinity)
1991	Andrew William Harvard Bunch
	(St Stephen's)
1998	Ainsley Laird Swift (St Stephen's)

Vicars of Old Windsor

1214	Richard Turk
1226	Mark Robert of Wynesham
	(Windlesham)
	Bartholomew deposed/
	deprived 1298
fl. 1325	Matthew
fl. 1366	William
fl. 1457	John Bylehar
fl. 1465	Richard Reynford
fl. 1545	John Robinson
1546	Thomas Eliot
1569	Robert Ashby -1578
1591	Henry Clark
1610	Richard Hamfrey 1647

There was no resident vicar from 1660 until
1700 as the benifice was too poor to support
one.

	Solomon Paysse
1693	Dr Anthony Mary de la Crosse
	(Dr la Croze)
1725	James Ferguson
1729	Thomas Smith
1736	Edward Ballard
1771	Thomas Fountains
1789	William Warrington

1824   Thomas Stephen Gossett (brother of Issac Gosset v. of Windsor)
1838   Henry John Cooper
1844   C. A. Steuart
1854   Arthur Cornish
1860   James St John Blount
1876   Thomas Eustace Harwood
1911   James Russell Napier
1928   William Francis Burnett Hoystead
1930   Albert Edward McCaig
1939   Philip Henry Douglas Ogle
1950   Arthur Grosvenor Coombs
1952   Thomas Herbert
1967   Eric Desmond Lewis
1973   Colin Paxton Aspell
1981   John Wedgewood Staples - 1996
1997   Nigel Pocock

Chairmen of Old Windsor Parish Council

1895   Lord Dunboyne
1907   Lt-Col. R.W. Follett
1921   Rev. J.R. Napier
1922   Mr W. Bullivant
1923   Rev. J.R. Napier
1924   Mr. A.P. Shaw
1949   Mr. C.W. Porter
1961   Mr A.F. Banks
1962   Mr I..J. Lacy
1963   Mr D. McKeown
1965   Mr C.W. Porter
1968   Mr L.S. Gentle
1970   Mr R.C. Knollys
1971   Dr R.A. Willis
1973   Mr H.G. Parker
1975   Mr A.H. Hartley
1977   Mr J.A. Morton
1979   Mr A.H. Hartley
1981   Mr C.J. Gilson
1983   Mr E. Wiles

1985   Mr M. Beer
1987   Mr R. Crawley to present.

All Saints' Dedworth

was staffed by curates from Clewer Church but in October 1911 the Curate in Charge is recorded as G B Budibent and in November A F Bliss. From then until July 1912 a number of curates and the Rector took services.

1912   E Clement Eddrup
1916   A T Gray
1917   E Keith Keily
1920   C N Wooler
1921   A J Clark
1923   H Clark (with W R Flex from June 1924)
1925   Bernard W Harvey and various others
1926   J H Jacques
1927   J Leighton Bailey
1928   E R J Henry
1930   F E Odell-Cheshire
1931   H E Wigglesworth
1932   R Cranston Garrett
1933   John R Simpson
1937   T R Parsons
1937   Charles Dunn
1938   E P Knight
1939   L F Williams
1941   A J C Turner
1942   Frank H Williams
1942   Donald Southeard
1945   Nawton Hall
1950   A R Methuen

Priest Missioners of the Conventional District of Dedworth

1957   A R Methuen
1976   John Anthony Stone

Vicars of the Parish of Dedworth

1982   John Anthony Stone
1986   Peter Duncan Atkinson
1993   Interregnum
1994   Louise Margaret Brown
           (priest in charge)
1996   Louise Margaret Brown (Vicar)
      The first Vicar to hold the
      Freehold of the Parish

Priests of St Agnes' Spital

1874   George H Swinny
1882   Henry Ley
1894   George Jones
1900   Herbert B Hunt
1903   Walter S Hulme
1904   Charles Farr
1911   Marsh Kirkby
1913   William Brook
1936   Richard E Beer
1939   Hubert T Trapp
1943   Alban C M Howard
1946   Edward A Dixon
1950   William A Pike
1950   Maurice W Hickin
1954   Brian P Elliot-Smith
1959   Frederick J Prebble
1963   Raymond G Hayne
1967   Graham A Friend
1975   Frederick T Bonham

Rectors of Holy Trinity

1844   Stephen Hawtrey
1852   Henry Hawtrey
1873   Arthur Robins
1900   Henry Tower
1945   Eric Dawson Walker (to 1972)
1973   Canon David Nigel Griffiths

Holy Trinity is now part of
New Windsor Team Ministry

Parish priests at the Roman Catholic Chapel in Hermitage Lane and St Edwards (from 1867)

1825   P A Comerbach
1830   T F Wilkinson
1854   Augustus Applegath
1889   John Longinetto
1936   Timothy Twomey
1957   William Kirk
1965   Timothy Dwyer
1979   Gerard Hetherington
1991   Michael Morrissey

Dedworth St Mark's Catholic Church Priests in Charge

1977   Fr Roger Hendry
1982   Fr Peter Codd
From 1985 the church has been
served from St Edward's in Windsor

Congregational Ministers

1804   Alexander Redford
1840   John Stoughton
1843   J B McCrea
1850   Joseph Augustus Miller
1855   James Macfarlane
1863   Samuel Eastman
1873   Thomas Orr
1893   Albert Lee
1906   Thomas Powell Landsdown
1914   George Felix Williams
1924   E Frank Tarrant (to 1946)
      Interregnum
1952   JS Dalton-Golding
1959   John Haile
1966   Donald Norwood

From 1972
United Reformed Church

1975 W Marshall-Jones
1978 Ivy Halden
1990 Derek Nuttall

Minsters of Windsor Baptist Church

1840 Rev Leslie
1840 Samuel Lillycrop
1863 Rev Gray
1869 Rev Swindell
1874 Rev Bourne
1877 Rev McMechan
1882 Rev Cole
1893 Rev Aubrey
1902 Rev Cunningham
1908 CH Sheen
1921 H James
1927 P Austen
1933 CS Hall
1937 A Collie
1942 AJ Barnard
1948 TL Cotes
1957 Joseph Sutton
1967 F Outen
1974 TH Lovegrove
1980 W Thomas
1983 Ken Paskin
1989 Brian Hankins
1992 G Marshall

Dedworth Baptist Church

1967 John Allen
1975 Peter Wilson
1990 Ian Randall (associate)
1991 Colin Jackson (student)
1992 Norman Cumming

Methodist Ministers

1815 Thomas Robinson
1817 John Scott
1819 George Dermott
1820 John Smith
1822 Richard Cooper
1824 Alexander Strachan
1827 William Pollard
1830 Joseph Walker
1831 Owen Rees
1832 John Stevens
1834 James Allen
1837 George Jackson
1840 James Brownell
1843 James Rosser
1846 John Nelson
1849 Samuel Young
1850 Joshua Mottram
1852 Thomas Turner
1855 John D Carey
1857 Samuel Young (again)
1860 Thomas Jeffries
1863 John Knowles
1866 Peter Samuel
1868 Joseph Portrey
1871 Charles Churchill
1873 John Bell
1874 George Penman
1877 Humphrey Hughes
1880 Henry L Church
1881 John Weatherill
1883 John Knowles
1886 John Westlake
1889 Rutland Spooner
1892 James D Tetley
1893 Daniel Pearson
1896 Jabez Iredale
1898 James F Pyle
1901 William Spiers
1904 Arthur E Sharpley
1907 Walter Seed

1910   E Percy Blackburn
1913   William Brook-Hirst
1916   J Samuel Hollingworth
1919   T Harold Bailey
1922   J Howard Weir
1925   T L B Westerdale
1928   E David Edwards
1929   Harold M Yates
1933   William E Passey
1937   V Donald Siddons
1940   Joseph Bonsall
1945   T Francis Glasson
1948   Robert Clemitson
1951   James H W Ingham
1956   J Leslie Hall
1963   Kenneth J Bate
1968   Alan Creber
1975   E Donald Mason
1980   Raymond G. Rowland
1988   James Booth
1998   Phyll Fanning

CALEYS

A department store of the
John Lewis Partnership

High Street, Windsor, Berkshire SL4 1LL
Tel: (01753) 863241   Email: caleys@johnlewis.co.uk

Local Studies facilities in WINDSOR

Need help with your research – step into Windsor Library!

- ❖ Local street directories from 1868-1974. (Do you know who lived in your house in the past?)
- ❖ Census returns from 1841-1891 for the Windsor area
- ❖ Windsor Express on microfilm from 1900 to date
- ❖ Cuttings file
- ❖ Photograph collection (can be copied according to copyright restrictions)
- ❖ Extensive collection of books relating to the Windsor area, including the Great Park and Forest. Also the Royalty Collection, books on monarchs with particular Windsor connections, but at least one on each monarch.
- ❖ Staff to help you find your way
- ❖ Microfilm reader/printer
- ❖ Photocopier

LIBRARY SERVICES
For details please contact the library on:
☎ **01753 743941** or email: **windsor.library@rbwm.gov.uk**

Royal Borough Museum Collection

Over 5,000 items in the Collection including:

- ❖ Archaeological finds
- ❖ Books, journals, newspapers and plans
- ❖ Costumes and coins
- ❖ Dioramas and documents
- ❖ Maps and medals
- ❖ Paintings, prints and photographs

From earliest times to yesterday.
Open Wednesdays by appointment.
Please contact the Curator.

☎ **(01628) 796829**
email:
museum.collection@ rbwm.gov.uk

Come and experience the
Town & Crown Exhibition
at the
Windsor Information Centre, 24 High Street, Windsor

This small exhibition uses audio-visual presentations to make this famous town's history come alive. See the influences of monarch's such as William the Conqueror, Henry VIII and Queen Victoria on the development of Windsor through the centuries.

Telephone:
(01628) 796829
Entry FREE of charge
Opening hours:
Daily Mon-Sat 10am-5pm
and Sun 10am-4pm

Select Bibliography

Windsor Local History

Abbreviations:

CSJB — Convent of St John the Baptist
OUP — Oxford University Press
OWGBC — Old Windsor Guide Book Committee
OWPC — Old Windsor Parish Council
RBNW — Royal Borough of New Windsor
RBWM — Royal Borough of Windsor and Maidenhead
WLHPG — Windsor Local History Publications Group

Baker, G.S., *Water Supply at Windsor*, unpublished chart, RBNW, 1966

Ballance, Selina, *Historic Windsor*, Jarrold Colour Publications, 1987

Berkshire Old and New, Journal of the Berkshire Local History Association

Bond, Maurice, *The Quincentenary Handbook*, St George's Chapel, 1975

—, *The Story of Windsor*, Local Heritage Books, 1984

Bond, Shelagh, *The First Hall Book of the Borough of New Windsor 1653-1725*, RBNW, 1968

Bonham, Valerie, *In the Midst of the People*, privately published, 1983

—, *A Joyous Service: The Clewer Sisters and their Work*, CSJB, 1989

—, *A Place in Life: The Clewer House of Mercy, 1849-83*, CSJB, 1992

—, *Sisters of the Raj: The Clewer Sister in India*, CSJB, 1997

Cullingham, Gordon, *The Royal Windsor Tapestry Manufactory 1876-1890*, RBWM, 1979

—, *Royal Windsor Stained Glass Manufactory*, RBWM, 1992

Cuthbert, Elizabeth, *Sixth Hall Book of the Borough of New Windsor*, RBWM, 1984

Farrer, Henry, *Windsor Town and Castle*, Phillimore & Co. Ltd, 1990

Garmonsway, G.N., *The Anglo-Saxon Chronicle*, Everyman, 1953

Gilson, C.J. *Old Windsor: A History of the Parish Council*, Manor Publications, 1981

— et al, *Old Windsor Handbook*, OWGBC, 1965

Gilson, Margaret, *Buildings of Old Windsor*, M.F.Gilson, 1995

—, *A Celebration of Old Windsor*, OWPC, 1995

Harwood, T.Eustace, *Windsor Old & New*, Harwood, 1929

Hawtrey, Rev. S., *An Account of St Marks School*, privately published, 1859

Hedges, David and Beryl, *Discover Windsor: Castle, Town and Park*, Luff Publications, 1971

Hedges, Beryl, *Exploring Windsor and Surroundings,* Thames Valley Hospice, undated

—, *Around Windsor in Old Photographs*, Sutton Publishing Ltd, 1998

— and Long, John, *The First Fifty Years of the Windsor and Eton Society*, undated

Hedley, Olwen, *Round and About Windsor and District*, Oxley & Son (Windsor) Ltd, 1948

Hibbert, Christopher, *The Court at Windsor: A Domestic History*, revised edition, Allen Lane, 1977

Holmes, Richard and Henton, G.M., *Windsor*, A. & C. Black, 1908

Hunter, Judith and Marson, Pamela, *The Changing Face of Windsor:The Beginnings*, WLHPG, 1977

Hunter, Judith, *From Tudor Inn to Trusthouse Hotel: The History of the Castle Hotel Windsor*, privately published, 1984

— et al, *The Streets of Windsor and Eton*, WLHPG, 1988

—, *Victorian Childhood in Windsor*, Madam Tussaud's, 1990

—, *Legislation, Royal Proclamations and other Directives relating to Inns, Taverns, Brandy Shops and Punch Houses*, doctoral thesis, Reading University, 1994

—, *A History of Berkshire*, Phillimore, 1995

—, *A History of the Windsor Guildhall, and a Guide to its Paintings and Treasures*, RBWM Leisure and Cultural Services, 2000

Knight, Charles (senior), *The Windsor Guide*, C. Knight, 1793

Langton, Jane, *The Second Hall Book of the Borough of New Windsor 1726-1783*, RBNW, 1973

Macnaghten, Angus, *Windsor in Victorian Times*, A. Macnaghten, 1975

—, *Windsor and Eton in Georgian Times*, A. Macnaghten, 1976

Middleton, Tom, *Royal Berkshire*, Barracuda, 1979

Mills, Michael, *How the Motor Bus came to Slough, Windsor and District 1904-14,* privately published, 2000

Morriss, Richard K., and Hoverd, Ken, *The Buildings of Windsor*, Alan Sutton, 1994

Over, Luke, *A Millennium in the Royal Borough*, RBWM, 1999

Potts, CR, *Windsor to Slough*, The Oakwood Press, 1993 *(railways)*

Roberts, Jane, *Views of Windsor*, Merrell Holberton, 1995

—, *Royal Landscape: The Gardens and Parks of Windsor*, 2 vols, Yale University Press, 1997

Rooney, Sheila, *Fires of Windsor Castle*, WLHPG, 1993

Rooney, Sheila and Pat, *St Leonards Hill: House, Hermitage and Hill*, Windsor Publications, 1991

Shaw, Denis, *Clewer: A Historical Miscellany*, privately published 1995

South, Raymond, *The Fifth Hall Book of the Borough of New Windsor*, RBNW, 1974

—, *The Book of Windsor: The Story of a Royal Town*, Barracuda Books Ltd, 1977

—, *Crown, College and Railways: How the Railways came to Windsor*, Barracuda, 1978

—, *Royal Castle, Rebel Town: Puritan Windsor in Civil War & Commonwealth*, Barracuda Books Ltd, 1981

Thomason, Geoff, *The Original Windsor: A History of Old Windsor*, G.G. Thomason, 1978

Tighe, R.R., and Davis, J.E., *Annals of Windsor*, 2 Vols, Longmans 1858

Underhill, Maitland, *Windsor as it Was*, Hendon Publishing Co. Ltd, 1972

Unknown, *Hippies and Hypocrisy*, Windsor Citizens Action Group, 1974

Victoria County History of Berkshire 1906-23

Windlesora 1-18, Journal of the WLHPG

Windsor Civic Week Official Brochure, RBNW 1966

Windsor Girls' School Diamond Jubilee, WGS. 1980

Biographies, Memoirs, etc

Boswell, James, *Life of Johnson*, OUP, 1969

Brewer, Derek, *The Life of Geoffrey Chaucer*, Oxford University Press, 1992

Burney, Fanny, *The Diary & Letters of Madame d'Arblay* (edited by Austin Dobson), Vols III & IV, Macmillan & Co.Ltd, 1904-05

Counsell, John, *Counsells Opinion*, Barrie & Rockliff, 1963

Cullingham, Gordon C., *F.J. Camm: the Practical Man 1895-1959*, G.C. Cullingham, 1996

Davenport, Hester, *Writers in Windsor*, Cell Mead Press, 1995

—, *Faithful Handmaid: Fanny Burney at the Court Of King George III*, Sutton Publishing Ltd, 2000

Dickens, Charles, *The Collected Letters*, edited by Madeline House and Graham Storey, OUP, Vol 2, 1969

Elliot, Alexander, *Journals*, Berkshire Record Office

Ellmann, Richard, *Oscar Wilde*, Hamish Hamilton, 1987

Evelyn, John, *The Diary of John Evelyn* (edited J. Bowle), OUP, 1983

Feeling, Keith, *Warren Hastings*, Macmillan & Co. Ltd, 1954

Fiennes, Celia, *The Journeys of Celia Fiennes* (edited John Hillaby), Macdonald & Co. Ltd, 1983

Hibbert, Christopher, *George III: A Personal History*, Viking, 1998

Holmes, Richard, *Shelley: The Pursuit*, Weidenfeld & Nicolson Ltd, 1974

Knight, Charles, *Passages of a Working Life during Half a Century*, Vol.1, Bradbury & Evans, 1864

Longford, Elizabeth, *Victoria R.I.*, Weidenfeld & Nicolson Ltd, 1964

Lear, Edward, *Selected Letters*, edited by Vivien Noakes, OUP, 1988

Lubbock, Constance A., *The Herschel Chronicle: The Life-Story of William Herschel and his sister Caroline*, Cambridge University Press, 1933

Maun, S., *Diary* (stationmaster), unpublished ms, RBWMC

Oliphant, Margaret, *The Autobiography of Margaret Oliphant*, (edited by Elizabeth Jay), OUP, 1990

Oxley, Norman, *AY Nutt: In Service to Three Monarchs at Windsor*, N.E. Oxley 1996

Pepys, Samuel, *The Diary of Samuel Pepys 1660-69* (abridged O.F. Morshead), G. Bell & Sons, 1972

Platt, Alan, *The Life and Times of Daniel Gooch*, Alan Sutton, 1987

Rooney, Sheila and Pat, *The Harcourt Journals: The Memoirs and diary of General Amédée and Sophia d'Harcourt* (edited and translated), WLHPG, 1998

Swift, Jonathan, *Journal to Stella*, edited by Harold Williams, OUP, 1974

Wells, H.G., *Experiment in Autobiography*, Victor Gollancz, 1934

Walpole, Horace, *Horace Walpoles Correspondence*, edited W.S. Lewis et al, OUP and Yale University Press, 1937-1983

Wordsworth, William and Dorothy, *The Early Letters*, edited by Ernest de Selincourt, OUP, 1935

Additional sources

Local directories, maps and surveys, documents held in the Royal Borough Museum Collection, Berkshire County Record Office, the Public Record Office, Windsor Library, parish magazines and church histories, the *Windsor, Slough & Eton Express*, the *Slough, Eton and Windsor Observer*, *Dictionary of National Biography* and other standard reference books, as well as the minutes of committee and council meetings of the Royal Borough of New Windsor and the Royal Borough of Windsor and Maidenhead.

Extensive use has also been made of the internet. Many local organisations have their own web sites and some include a page giving the history of the organisation.

Windsor Local History Publications Group

Windlesora

Copies of Windlesora 1-7 are no longer available from the group, but can be consulted at Windsor Library and are sometimes available second hand. The following are still available.

No 8 (£1.50) Samuel Lillycrop, Canon Carter and the 'Clewer Case', Prince Consort Cottages, Some Windsor Memorials, Stained Glass Windows with Windsor Connections.

No 9 (£1.50) Davies of Windsor, Clockmakers, J. Gane and Co of Eton, Old Windsor Cricket, Football and Working Men's Club, Bier Lane

No 10 (£1.75) Windsor's Riverside, Poor Little Orphans (St John's Home), Joseph Ryder, The First UK Airmail Delivery, Windsor Steam Laundry, Royal Volunteer Review.

No 11 (£2) Robert Keayne of Windsor and Massachusetts, Clewer St Stephens's, Fred Fuzzens' Early Life, Windsor Parish Players, A Schoolboy View of the 1947 Floods, Sophie Elizabeth, Marquise d'Harcourt.

No. 12 (£2) Margaret Oliphant, Cinderella in the Waterloo Chamber, St Augustines Home Clewer, The Chocolate Connection (Caleys).

No 13 (£2) Windsor Boys' School, Bachelors' Acre Tank, Princess Christian Hospital, WG Grace and Cumberland Lodge, Clewer Camera Club, Edward Lear at Clewer Green.

No 14 (£2) Lord Gowrie VC, Windsor Model Aero Club, The Ken Shepherd Archive, Dedworth War Memorial (Belford Alexender Wallis Wilson), "Curtain Up" - The Theatre Royal Programme.

No 15 (2.75) **Our Twenty First Birthday Issue** Mary 'Perdita' Robinson, Theatre Royal and the National Trust, William Morris Stained Glass at Dedworth Church, Alice in Wonderland - the Windsor Connection, Topham Foote and Thomas Reeve, Memoires of the Marquis d'Harcourt, Rise and fall of the Windsor Bank, Harry Greenwood VC, Problems at Queen Victoria's Funeral.

No 16 (£2.75) Our Pretty Witty Nell (Gwyn), Edward Matthew Ward RA, The Children's Tragedy, Perambulations of the Parish Boundary 1801, White Bus to Winkfield, Old Windsor Carnival, The Apothecary's Token 1666, Pennyroyal Almshouses.

No 17 (£2.75) Market Cross House, Who Tried to Kill Lady Florence Dixie? Esther Sheridan, Windsor Deceived (Windsor's Hospitals under the NHS), The Beautiful Lady Waldegrave, Lady Florence Paget, From Workhouse to Mansion, Living in the Shadow of Eton College, A Suffragette Attack, The Windsor Chair, Oliver Brooks VC, Congregationalism in Windsor - The Beginnings,

No 18 (£2.75) Passages of a Working Life - Charles Knight, The Creators of the Dioramas, St Peter's School Old Windsor, Denman and Goddard, Mrs Horace Dodge and St Leonard's Mansion, Eton Wick - a Village in the Shadow of Eton, The Reverend Arthur Robins, MA, Debunking a Myth - The Copper Horse.

Copies of *Windlesora* and *The Streets of Windsor and Eton* (£2) can be obtained from the group at 256 Dedworth road, Windsor SL4 4JR. Please enclose 50p for postage and packing if necessary.

Windsor Local History Publications Group